LOWELL D. STREIKER

◄◄◄

The Gospel of Irreligious Religion

Insights for Uprooted Man from Major World Faiths

SHEED AND WARD : NEW YORK

© Sheed and Ward, Inc., 1969

Library of Congress Catalog Card Number 75–82603

Standard Book Number 8362–0290–2

Quotations from Making It by Norman Podhoretz © Copyright 1967 by Norman Podhoretz reprinted by permission of Random House Inc.

Manufactured in the United States of America

To Great Teachers
Zenos Hawkinson, Samuel Klein, Bernard Phillips

Contents

PREFACE ix

INTRODUCTION xi

Part One: The Man of Faith and the Challenge
of Other Religions 3
1 The Encounter of Religions in a Rapidly
Changing World 5
2 The Hindu Attitude toward Other Religions 37

Part Two: Mysticism and Modern Man 63
3 The Religion of the Hippies 65
4 The Buddha's Path of Selfless Ecstasy 87

Part Three: The Legitimacy of Religious Irreligion 113
5 How to Be a Jewish Atheist 115
6 The Religious Irreligion of Rabindranath
Tagore 141

RECOMMENDED READINGS 161

Preface

THE AUTHOR acknowledges his special debts to his colleagues in the Department of Religion, Temple University; Tom and Mary Lynne Bird for unceasing inspiration; Louis Del Soldo, a graduate student who has taught me much; Murray F. C. Goldman for the attentions of a good heart and a clear mind; Philip Scharper, for encouragement to undertake and pursue this volume; my wife and children for patient understanding; and, of course, to the many undergraduate and graduate students at Temple University with whom I have discussed these subjects during the past five years.

Introduction

NEAR THE END of his illustrious career, Paul Tillich became convinced that a new kind of theology was needed. He expressed a hope that in the future the structure of religious thought would be determined by an interpenetration of the religions of mankind. Tillich realized that his own efforts, like those of all previous Christian theologians, had reflected presuppositions and prejudices based on in-depth experience of only one religious community. Tillich's long and fruitful career was dedicated to the task of relating the timeless symbols of Christian faith to the fundamental human issues of the twentieth century. But Tillich was aware that he had labored within a single "circle of faith."

Shortly before his death, Tillich declared that the religious isolation in which traditional theology had developed was obsolete. He encouraged Christians to formulate their basic religious experiences in a "universally valid" manner by relating these experiences to spiritual discoveries of other men. He rejected the notion that such openness to the experiences which lie in the depths of every concrete religion would produce "an all-embracing abstraction which would destroy religion as such."[1] For he knew that the universality of religion resides in a common humanity rather than an ideal synthesis of metaphysical assertions and ethical maxims.

In the place of Christian *summas* such as his own monumental *Systematic Theology*, Tillich proposed "a theology taking into consideration not only the existential crisis and the religious vacuum of contemporary Western societies, but also the religious traditions of Asia and the primitive world, together with their recent crises and traumatic transformations."[2] This book is intended as a contribution to just such a theology.

Theology is a generalist discipline. It is the attempt to see *all things in relation to God and God in terms of all things*. The more thoroughly the theologian understands the world in which he lives and works, the more adequate is his vision of the divine. But the world of man cannot be comprehended by a single mind. Therefore, the theologian must recognize the limitations of his perspective and acknowledge his basic dependence upon those who investigate man and his world with the methodological tools of such disciplines as sociology, anthropology, depth psychology, history, political science, economics, etc. Moreover, the theologian will also look for clues in cultural productions (novels, plays, poetry, motion pictures, and music), for art proclaims man's self-understanding and sense of relation to the ultimate with an unparalleled clarity, intensity and universality.

There is one academic discipline, in addition to those just mentioned, which would seem of immense value to the theologian. I am referring to the methodological approach variously described as "the scientific study of religions," "the history of religions," "phenomenology of religion," "comparative religions," and "religious historical studies." This discipline interprets man on the basis of one of his unique activities—his religion. Although the theological significance of such investigation is obvious, the data of the scholarly study of the religions of man is rarely utilized. This book is based on the conviction that the time has come for theologians to become phenomenologists of religion and for historians of religions to become theologians. Attempting to interpret and systematize the affirmations of one's own faith without investigating the nature of the experiences from which they have arisen is rather like studying German without reference to the history, literature, and culture of the German people. Likewise, restricting one's endeavors to cataloging and documenting the responses of mankind to fundamental issues upon which our survival depends without actively participating in the struggle for authentic humanity or world community may be scholarly, but it is neither human nor responsible.

The infection known as academic specialization—the atomization of the world of man into dozens of conflicting, unrelated "departments" of study—is the chief cause of dissatisfaction on the college campus and the major reason for the final triviality of intellectual pursuits. By dismembering man into irreconcilable fields of study, the university creates a *disuniversity*. The student is bombarded, confused, and disoriented. He is left groping for meaning, for significance, for humanity. Even more lamentable than the theologian's ignorance of the nature of religion is the avoidance of the religious dimension of human experience by devotees of other scholarly disciplines. How, we must ask, is it possible to understand Arab history without a knowledge of Islam? Or the ideological foundations of Western sociopolitical institutions without reference to Hebraic ethical monotheism? Or the current political crises in Southeast Asia apart from an appreciation of the influence of Buddhism? Further, how can one explain Marxism without describing the bourgeois Christianity in reaction to which it arose? How can a psychologist enter into a therapeutic relationship without probing the religious factors which contribute to the formation of his patient's personality?

As a phenomenologist of religious experience, I am concerned with the nature of religion, the various responses to what man regards as central to his existence, and the manner in which the rare moments of personally transforming bliss are synthesized with the mundane experiences of the everyday. Quite often I turn to such disciplines as sociology, psychology, linguistics, and cultural criticism for the tools necessary for the interpretation of man's religious quest. Since religious experience is always part of the total life of

an individual or a group, my work would be hamstrung
without the overlapping insights of my academic colleagues.
I am dependent upon them for knowledge of the social,
political, psychological, historical, and other relevant factors which shape and color the religious response to reality.

These factors are never absent from religious experience.
But they are neither the only nor the most significant elements. Religious experience is the awareness of something
ultimate in power and meaning, of something holy or divine
upon which all beings depend, of an extraordinary other
which transcends, judges, and yet sustains the world of
mundane experience. It is the encounter with this mysterious but ineludible "something" which is the basis of all
religious activity—even though such activity is conditioned
by the circumstances of the individual's existence.

In this book I attempt to elucidate several religious
phenomena. However, interpretation is not my primary
purpose. First and foremost, this work is a *theological* essay. It grows out of a personal attempt to grasp the world
—a world shaped by religious, a-religious, and antireligious
influences—through participation as well as reflection. But
more fundamentally, this book expresses the impact upon
the writer's consciousness of several interrelated, interacting,
and inseparable factors: (a) the current ferment within traditional religions; (b) the crises of contemporary life in its
personal, social, and political dimensions; (c) the unprecedented encounter of the world's religions; (d) the secu-
larist's rejection of all religion.

As participant in and victim of a world of rapid change, of increasing personal alienation, of mounting dissatisfaction with religion both within and without the traditional circles of faith, of revolutionary chaos and moral devaluation, of wars and rumors of wars—in such a world I join my efforts to those by men of many faiths to seek after God. I use the word "God" for convenience, regarding it as shorthand for the problem of our times. "God" is employed in my projected theology to represent the hoped for, sought after, unrealized answer to the quandary: What is the meaning of the personal life, social existence, and existential world of man? Realizing full well the narrowness of my purview, as a single man stranded on his personal spatio-temporal island, I am trying to discover universal principles, underlying unity, and final design in my world and my times—admitting all the while that this quest may be hopeless, that the answer may turn out to be "There is no answer."

Of one thing I am convinced. No individual can do more than sharpen the issues, rephrase the problems, reformulate the dilemmas, remove a few of the obstacles. Therefore, I devote the first part of this book to a consideration of the major obstructions. I argue that knowledge of one manifestation of the Spirit is knowledge of none. In the current crisis of confidence, Christians should turn for guidance to those who have pursued the discipline of the religious life far longer and more steadfastly than they. For even more important than the emergence of a broader ecumenism involving all the religions of mankind are the lessons which world religions hold for uprooted moderns—particularly the young. It is to their discontent and disillusionment that I direct these lessons in the remaining chapters.

In chapter three, an analysis of the drug-induced mysticism of the Hippies is offered. The following chapter relates the message of the Buddha to the contemporary spiritual situation. These two chapters are joined together under the rubric "Mysticism and Modern Man." Although the two chapters are intended to illumine one another, I have purposely left many of the implications to the reader.

The concluding part, "The Legitimacy of Religious Irreligion," develops the thesis that irreligion and atheism are the most appropriate *religious* responses to the present situation. However, the "irreligion" proposed must not be confused with the cynical rejection of that which the individual never previously possessed. chapter five, "How to Be a Jewish Atheist," examines the striving after religious identity and dissatisfaction with institutional religion of the Jewish intellectual. Lest this chapter win the author the accusation of anti-Semitism, let me state that the Jewish identity crisis differs neither in degree nor intensity from the turmoil within other religious communities: Muslim, Buddhist, Hindu, Christian, and even secular humanist. I have chosen Judaism to articulate this problem because

(a) I am a Jew and, thus, have personally experienced the dilemma of religious identity as a Jew; (b) the majority of my students have been Jewish—and mostly rootless, searching Jews at that; (c) Jewish writers have documented the subject with a sensitivity so far unequalled by others. No service is done the Jewish people by the avoidance of such a pressing issue.

In the last chapter, "The Religious Irreligion of Rabindranath Tagore," an outstanding Indian poet-philosopher is chosen to illustrate a religiously affirmative irreligion. This chapter also seeks to bring Tagore a measure of the attention which he deserves but which has been denied him in contemporary America. Other figures could have been selected as examples of a fervent devotion to a reality available to man *in, through,* and *despite* religion. Martin Buber, Paul Tillich, and Pierre Teilhard de Chardin were considered. But in the end I chose the religious thinker who, in my judgment, speaks the most directly, eloquently, and universally.

Finally, I extend an invitation. This book grew out of hundreds of conversations—discussions with Hindus, Buddhists, Christians, Jews, Muslims, secularists, religious sceptics, Marxists, hardnosed pragmatists, Black Nationalists, Hippies, New Leftists, and embedded establishmentarians. (My years with the amazing Temple University Department of Religion have kept me at a number of exciting crossroads.) I hope that new discussions, new opportunities for cooperative effort, new channels for spiritual creativity will follow.

Shall we talk further?

LOWELL D. STREIKER
Philadelphia, Pennsylvania
April, 1969

NOTES

[1] Jerald C. Brauer, ed., "The Significance of the History of Religions for the Systematic Theologian," *The Future of Religions* (New York: Harper Row, 1966), p. 94.

[2] Mircea Eliade, "Paul Tillich and the History of Religions," a memorial tribute included in *The Future of Religions*, p. 31. The implications of Tillich's proposal for the future of theology are examined within the context of his total life's work in my dissertation, *The Mystical A Priori: Paul Tillich's Critical Phenomenology of Religion* (Princeton: Princeton University, 1968).

THE GOSPEL OF
IRRELIGIOUS
RELIGION

Part One

<<<<<<<<<<<<

THE
MAN OF FAITH
AND
THE CHALLENGE OF
OTHER
RELIGIONS

1

≪≪≪≪≪≪≪≪≪≪≪≪≪≪≪≪≪≪≪≪≪≪≪≪≪≪≪≪≪≪≪≪≪≪≪≪≪≪≪

The Encounter of Religions in a Rapidly Changing World

THERE IS LITTLE DOUBT in my mind that the twenty-first century will look back upon our age and its accomplishments much as Charles Dickens recalled the era of revolution in which he set his great historical novel, *A Tale of Two Cities.* According to Dickens, the last quarter of the eighteenth century was ". . . . the best of times, it was the worst of times, it was the age of wisdom, it was the age of foolishness, it was the epoch of belief, it was the epoch of incredulity, it was the season of Light, it was the season of Darkness, it was the spring of hope, it was the winter of despair, we had everything before us, we had nothing before us. . . ."

In 1892 my grandfather's realization that there was nothing before him in the ghettoes of the Baltic and everything before him in the New World led him to Chicago, the site of the spectacular Columbian Exposition. During the

5

seventy-three years of his life in America, he witnessed an outpouring of technological advances, human catastrophes, political transformations, cultural transitions, and social upheavals without parallel in the history of mankind. He toiled to raise and educate his four sons and two daughters during years of peace and plenty, through times of war and want. When my grandfather was a young man, the automobile—formerly the plaything of the rich and eccentric—suddenly supplanted the horse and radically altered the pattern of family existence. Shortly before I, his first grandchild, was born, the airplane firmly established its place as a major means of transportation coast to coast and continent to continent. When he died in 1965, man was already poking about the fringes of outer space.

The more than eighty years of my grandfather's life were but a moment in the millions of years of human history. Yet the brief span of his life saw the birth of a plethora of epochs—the air age, the jet age, the atomic age, the computer age, the cybernetics age, the space age, to name but a few. His lifetime encompassed the introduction of radio, motion pictures, television, antibiotics, heart transplants, artificial kidneys, radar, psychiatry, and plastics. He was born in a part of the world coveted by imperial Russia, the Austro-Hungarian Empire, and the Prussian monarchy. The Russia of the tsars was soon to become the Soviet Union of Lenin and Stalin. The domains of Emperor Franz Joseph would become a gaggle of independent nations. The Germany of the kaisers would be in turn a democracy, an all-conquering neopagan dictatorship, a spoil of war divided among her conquerors, and two separate nations.

My grandfather came to a boisterous, self-confident, expansive, and aggressive America. A quarter of a century after his arrival, his adopted nation would have to intervene in a war among the European powers. For the first time in history, Europe would be unable to solve its own problems. America would intrude, intending "to end all wars." In fact, she would end the determination of world history by the contending European empires. For not only would Britain, France, Germany, Russia and the other belligerents lose a generation of young men in the trenches of France, the forests of Poland, and the alpine passes of Italy, but European culture, religion, morality, and social stratification would receive mortal wounds as well.

The twentieth century began as "the Christian Century" —a designation which still appears in an utterly unconvincing manner as the name of a leading Protestant weekly. This was to have been the century of progress, i.e., the era in which the benefits of civilization, technology, and self-confident Christianity were to spread across the face of the globe, eradicating superstition and suffering, establishing law and morality, banishing illiteracy, and tribalism. But, alas, the age of faith in human achievement, the era of loyalty to God, country, and one's station and its duties, is increasingly becoming the post-Christian, post-bourgeois, and post-European age. The religion, nationalism, materialism, technology, and socio-economic stratification of the West no longer form a single, unitary system of values which must be accepted *in toto* to assure the advancement of the race. The stresses and strains of the modern age have left all mankind with doubts, dilemmas, and a wholesale distrust of the platitudes of the past.

The first two-thirds of this century were a veritable age of revolutions, as transformation followed transformation in bewildering succession. The last third of this century may prove to be an age of relativization, a period in which all the so-called gains of the past several decades are called in question, in which the contradictions between what we believe and the way we live are ruthlessly exposed. The worldwide unrest of the young is evidence of this process. If I may cite a rather homely example, consider the spread of marijuana among American youth.

The use of marijuana, a relatively harmless sedative, has been illegal for thirty years. Possession and sale of "pot" or "grass"—as the drug is known among the young—are criminal offenses which carry extremely stringent penalties. Despite vigorous attempts to enforce these laws (e.g., nearly six hundred marijuana arrests in Philadelphia during 1967), marijuana is readily available to anyone who cares to obtain it. The majority of the bright, outgoing students with whom I come into contact have experimented with "pot" on at least one occasion. On the basis of a study which he conducted of high school marijuana users, Dr. Herbert Blumer, chairman of the sociology department of the University of California at Berkeley, observes that most are outstanding in both academic and extra-curricular pursuits. Upon his return from Army service in Vietnam, John Steinbeck IV, son of the late novelist, testified before a Senate subcommittee that three-quarters of the men with whom he had served used marijuana.

In part, the spread of pot may be traced to the impatient, undisciplined hedonism of the young. The frenzied quest after "pleasure, NOW," rather than the long-term satisfactions which attend a "socially productive" life, characterizes the rambunctious minority which manages to grab the headlines and the television coverage. In part the marijuana user is engaging in the rebellion of youth against adult authority which is repeated in every generation. The disdain of the young for their elders and the resentment of youth by the old are among the most ancient and persistent themes in the literature of all people, in all nations, at all times. Plato speaks for the young of every period when he observes: "Solon was under a delusion when he said that a man when he grows old may learn many things— for he can no more learn much than he can run much; youth is the time for any extraordinary toil" (The Republic, Book VII, 536-D, Jowett trans.). Yet the same author's advice to the young breathes the sentiment of every elder generation: "You are young, my son, and, as the years go by, time will change and even reverse many of your present opinions. Refrain therefore awhile from setting yourself up as a judge of the highest matters" (Laws, 888, Jowett).

But experimentation with drugs such as marijuana is

much more than an instance of the general tendency of the young to disregard the counsel of adult authority. The popularity of marijuana is symptomatic of a deep-seated alienation between two cultures. For many young people, the use of pot is, to be sure, nothing more than a tame, immature prank, much like the conspicuous petting and drinking of earlier adolescents (including their own parents). But unlike previous shenanigans, the use of pot stems in large measure from a fundamental distrust of both adult advice and the values which motivate this advice. Earlier adolescent mischief stemmed from an eagerness to enjoy such "adult only" pleasures as sex, alcohol, and tobacco. Panty raids, teenage drinking, and smoking behind the barn expressed an impatience with the period between childhood and adult life. But pot smoking is patently anti-social. A large number of young adults have discovered through their own experience that the arguments against the use of marijuana are fallacious. They know that the vast majority of marijuana users do not go on to more dangerous, addictive drugs such as heroin; that marijuana, unlike alcohol, does not cause organic harm to the body; that pot smoking does not lead to crime or sexual promis-cuity. They feel that the persecution of marijuana users, the imposition of penalties equivalent to those for the pos-session and use of heroin, is arbitrary and irrational. The young suspect that the singling out of marijuana for proscriptions by an adult society which is dependent upon numerous drugs—stimulants, relaxants, analgesics, anti-

histamines, contraceptive pills, antibiotics—reflects a fundamental prejudice against the young and a desire to deprive
the young of pleasures which are no more harmful than
universally accepted adult indulgences. In the words of Dr.
Joel Fort, a psychiatrist who has served on a number of
national and international commissions concerned with
drug abuse:

> We live in a drug-ridden society. Marijuana is just one of
> our drugs, and like the rest, it has some bad effects. In
> short-term, small-dose use, it shares the short-term, small-
> dose dangers of alcohol: people lose some of their co-
> ordination—they ought not to drive or handle dangerous
> equipment while under the influence of marijuana or al-
> cohol. . . . we can't be hypocritically selective about our
> concern, condemning other people's favorite drugs but re-
> fusing to be equally stringent about our own. If we get
> down to basics, we can't sincerely work on lessening mari-
> juana use without trying to lessen the use of alcohol, or
> even tobacco and coffee.[1]

The most telling objection to the spread of marijuana is
that the habitual pot smoker ceases to be "socially productive"—that he ignores his appearance, loses interest in his
studies, becomes noncompetitive and passive. But, demand
the current generation of young adults, what is "social
productivity"? Must passivity, introspection, lack of aggression, and disregard for conventional modes of dress be
regarded as socially dysfunctional? Have their elders found

peace of mind or contentment in the remorseless, acquisitive rat race? Have the parents of today's malcontents been able to cope with increased leisure time, earlier retirement, and freedom from want? A home in the suburbs, two automobiles, a color television, orthodontia for the children— is this the chief end of man? Does not the overstimulated adult world—a world beset with ulcers, a high divorce rate, mental illness, intergroup rancor, crime, war, environmental pollution, overpopulation, and the individual's gnawing sense of being lost in the mass—yearn for the right to be occasionally less than "socially productive"?

I am not claiming that the marijuana user has any better answer to the problems of modern life than his success-oriented elders. Chronic under-achievement is as self-defeating as relentless over-achievement. But I am suggesting that the vehemence of adult opposition to youthful experimentation with marijuana stems in large measure from adult frustration with their own world as well as the vague feeling that there is something antisocial about today's young people. If "antisocial" means unenamored with the prospects of losing one's identity in industrialized urban society, then these suspicions are not unfounded. But adult intolerance of the follies of the young arises not so much from the social threat of such antics as from adult dissatisfaction with their own lot. The unpardonable sin of today's youth is that they hold up the mirror. It is from our own image that we recoil—not from them.

Actually there is no generation gap—despite what we

read in the mass circulation weekly magazines. There is a basic division among men which has little to do with age. Modern life separates us into two groups—the vast, grey army of conformists and the noisy minority of rebellious individualists. The nameless, faceless mass allows itself to be folded, spindled, and mutilated in hopes of security, advancement, and acceptability. This mediocre majority is constantly plagued by the protests of those who resist the process of standardization. The rebels are a motley collection with no unifying principles. They include those who have been denied a share in the benefits of the mass age as well as those who have not yet attained status in institutional power structures—particularly the poor, the black, and the young. Frustration, deprivation, powerlessness, and disillusionment combine according to the alchemy of dissent and produce specters of chaos which haunt the consciousness of the defenders of the status quo.

The crisis of relativization threatens every value structure and every community—secular or religious—based upon a value structure. Marxist socialism is no less challenged by its internal critics than American democracy is by its malcontents. Self-sufficient, technological secularism attacks not only the theistic religions of the West but Oriental traditions and even humanism as well. Such circumstances call for a pooling of spiritual and economic resources, for the creation of a human community which can withstand the inhumane, depersonalizing pressures of modern life.

The mass age is an unparalleled opportunity for a revolution in the relations of the religions of man. Technological advances in the fields of communication and transportation not only bring us into ever more intimate contact with one another but reveal that Christian, Muslim, Jew, Hindu, and Buddhist are confronted with identical dilemmas. The problems of the modern age—the growing depersonalization of life in urban culture, the breakdown of traditional patterns of personal and social life, the estrangement of man from his environment, overpopulation, political unrest and social upheaval (particularly among the young), the threat of a thermonuclear holocaust which would totally erase man and his achievements from the face of this planet —these problems bind all men together in a community of concern. But so far it has only been the problems which have united us. Among those most devoted to ultimate issues—religious men and women—there has been little actual concerted effort or conversation.

As the distinguished Japanese Buddhist, Masao Abe, maintains, ours is a time in which all religions are being exposed to the devastating attacks of a-religious and anti-religious forces. Marxism, scientism (faith in technology as the ultimate savior of mankind), hedonism, materialism, aggressive nationalism and the other forces of self-sufficient secularism are eroding away the very foundations of religion itself. As desirable as a spirit of tolerance between the religions of the world may be, it is hardly sufficient to meet the challenge of modern secularism. In Abe's opinion,

What is needed is rather an opening up of a new spiritual horizon throughout the East and the West which provides room for the religions, no more bound by their traditional patterns, to face jointly the common problem of man, the problem of man's self-estrangement. For precisely this is the most serious problem of our time—that man can no more trust himself and hence finds himself in the vacuum of meaninglessness.[2]

The present situation demands of the Christian a willingness to listen as well as to speak. If men of different faiths are unable to communicate with one another, there is little prospect that they will be able to communicate with the nonreligious (often antireligious) secular world. Dialogue provides the participants opportunity for (1) honest, charitable argument through which one may encounter numerous categories of faith and practice which a given tradition may have ignored; (2) reflection and self-understanding as one is forced to explain and defend his own faith; (3) the stripping away of nonessentials: cultural associations, institutionalized forms, theological cliches; and (4) cooperation in dealing with the fundamental problems of modern life.

Although many Christians recognize the advantages of cooperation (see the discussion of the Second Vatican Council's Declaration on Non-Christian Religions below), they still regard the conversion of the non-Christian as the major goal of interreligious conversations. Indeed it would be possible to number on the fingers of one hand recognized

Christian leaders who have conceived the possibility of a meeting of world religions from which Christianity could benefit as well as to which it could contribute.

What I am proposing is a Christian attitude of openness to the religions of other men, a willingness to learn from non-Christians, an appreciation of the convictions and conventions which govern the daily lives of Hindus, Buddhists, Muslims and others. I am advocating the study by Christians of non-Christian religions and the collaboration of Christians with adherents of other traditions. Such encounter must be regarded not as a form of covert evangelism but as an opportunity to bind man to man through mutual sympathy, respect, and understanding. As Trude Weiss-Rosmarin, a leading Jewish journalist, states: "Now there is nothing wrong with missionary efforts. A strong conviction and eagerness to win converts for it are complementary. It is objectionable, however, when the missionary intention and aim are concealed and masked. The Jewish hatred and contempt for Christian missions to Jews are so intense because the missionaries hide their true colors."[3]

In dialogue I persuade the Hindu to look upon life in the Christian way, and he persuades me to look upon life in his way. This is far different from my attempting to make a Christian of him or his attempting to make a Hindu of me. In evangelism, the Hindu becomes a Christian. In dialogue, I become a Hindu. Imaginatively, empathetically, I discover what it is like to live within his skin. And yet I maintain my faithfulness to my own tradition. As the Christian participant declares in Ninian Smart's *A Dialogue of Religions,* "I give notice that however Hindu I may be, I shall remain a Hindu Christian!"[4]

CHRISTIAN ATTITUDES TOWARD OTHER RELIGIONS

Throughout the world, present cooperative activities between adherents of different religions are usually non-religious in purpose and sponsorship. Organizations such as the United Nations, UNICEF, the Red Cross, and the National Conference of Christians and Jews unite men and women in joint efforts *despite* their diverse religious heritages. Seldom have Christians, Jews, Muslims, Hindus, and Buddhists been able to work together *precisely* as Christians, Jews, Muslims, Hindus, and Buddhists. A major obstacle to cooperation between the religions of mankind has been the inhospitable attitudes of Christianity toward other religions. Contemporary Christian responses to non-Christian religions range from implacable hostility toward the alien (an attitude which is certain to drive away the non-Christian) to uncritical acceptance of the novel merely because of its novelty (a stance which produces suspicion and distaste on the part of orthodox churchmen). A brief sketch of contemporary Christian reactions to the religions of others will indicate the dimensions of the problem.

RADICAL DISPLACEMENT

At one end of the scale stands the rigorist who regards all non-Christian religions as so many feeble, human attempts to come to terms with the divine. The rigorist responds to religions other than his own with an attitude of war. The non-Christian is a prey to be captured, a benighted soul waiting to be led to the light. Non-Christian religions are regarded as systems of error, idolatry, and immorality invented by sinful man as deliberate obstacles to encounter with God.

The rigorist warns that contact with world religions exposes the Christian to the danger of losing sight of the uniqueness of his own faith and minimizes the discontinuity of human *religions* and divine *revelation*. For, according to the rigorist, the Gospel is revelation *sui generis*. All *religions*, including "Christianity," must be condemned as futile, human inventions. The rigorist recognizes that man is "the religious animal," but to him "religious" means apostate. Man's heart is an idol factory. Man can arrive at the goal intended for him by God not by continuing along the way indicated by his religion but only by radically breaking away from it.

Even the Christian religion must be rejected qua religion. According to the rigorist, the tendency to confuse Christianity (the religion) with the Gospel (God's saving message to mankind) results in the falsification of the Gospel and the misunderstanding of its relation to non-Christian religion. Not even the Christian can take refuge in his religion. For Christianity is only a corrupt, man-inspired attempt to come to terms with the Gospel. And when the Gospel enters a person's life, the old way (including all religious association) is completely swept away. "If any man be in Christ, he is a new creature. Old things are passed away . . ." (Rom. 12:1–2).

The rigorist offers the adherent of another religion only one possible choice—the radical displacement of your faith by mine. Obviously, theories of radical displacement are part of the missionary's arsenal. The only reason that a Christian should be interested in non-Christian religion is tactical—so that he may know his enemy. But even such study is fraught with peril. For who can predict what errors may creep into the missionary's soul as the result of his exposure to apostasy.

In the mind of the rigorist there is no truth in any non-Christian religion which is not already in the Gospel. Those few truths which are contained in these religions are conserved and perpetuated only by the true faith. For in their natural state these goods are so intertwined with untenable elements (e.g., polytheism and idolatry) that they weaken the very systems of which they are a part. In the words of a Roman Catholic missionary to Japan: "There is no truth anywhere which is not already in Christ, and in Christ in its richest and fullest form. The Gospel offers all that the Vedanta, the Koran, the Lotus Sutra or the Kojiki offer, and infinitely more. Christ includes all teachers, sages and all prophets."[5] Thus, not only is it dangerous for the Christian to encounter religions other than his own, it is really unnecessary.

UNIVERSALISM

Theories of religious universalism or syncretism encourage an attitude diametrically opposed to the "my truth versus your error" stance of the advocates of radical displacement. The syncretistic notion that a universal religion can be constructed which includes beliefs, ethical maxims, and ceremonies selected from the major world religions exercises a perennial appeal—particularly to men and women who feel themselves without rootage in the religion of their childhood. The universalist insists: "Since all religions share the same fundamental beliefs in a supreme being and the value of the good life, why should there be so many religions? Isn't the lesson of the past clear enough—many religions create many enmities? Doesn't the spread of irreligion require that religious men of all communities pool their resources to provide for a common defense?"

The argument of the universalist reminds one of the message of Cecil B. de Mille's extravaganza, *The Crusades*, which turns up on late-night television now and then. The heroine, Berengaria of Navarre (portrayed by Loretta

Young), interposes herself between the leaders of the belligerents, Richard the Lionhearted and Saladin, with a saccharine plea for peace. Why should Christian and Muslim kill one another, she asks, just because they disagree on whether the divine should be called "God" or "Allah"? After all, what's in a name? But what de Mille and all universalists overlook is that religious differences are functions of cultural, political, racial, and many other differences. The Crusades were inspired as much by the mercantile aspirations of the various Italian centers of commerce and the prospects of new lands to relieve the overcrowding of Frankish domains as they were by Christian outrage at Muslim control of Jerusalem. The sack of Christian Constantinople by the armies of the Fourth Crusade plainly demonstrates the insignificance of the religion of the Crusaders compared to their lust for booty as a motivational factor. And yet the Crusades were religious wars. If the French (who did most of the fighting) and their erstwhile allies had not been at least nominally Christians and their enemies had not been in some sense Muslims, there would have been no such conflicts. For it took the power of a common faith to end the internecine feuds among the rival princes of Europe and among their counterparts, the sultans of Islam. The control of Jerusalem, a city which is sacred to many religions, thus provided a unifying issue as well as a religiously sanctioned excuse for Christians and Muslims (particularly the former) to indulge propensities for inhumanity contrary to the spirit of all religion.

Like all human undertakings, the Crusades were ambiguous. Neither the religion nor the irreligion of the combatants fully explains these hostilities. Religion does not exist in abstracto but only in, through, and often despite the lives of men. For religion is an individual's response to that which he experiences as ultimate, as most valuable, as dearest to himself, as most real and intense. Religion is not a special activity set apart from all other human involvements. It is a man's relationship to ultimate reality in his specific, socio-economical-historical context. Sometimes an individual's religion is derived from and underwritten by that context; sometimes his religion operates at variance with the values of the age and society in which he lives. Much of the time there are subtle tensions between the individual's religion and the society in which he lives, just as there are recurrent strains between religious and social institutions.

Religion is a dynamic living with the gap between the way things ought to be and the way they are. As Alfred North Whitehead declares:

Religion is the vision of something which stands behind and within the passing flux of immediate things; something which is real, and yet waiting to be realized; something which is a remote possibility, and yet the greatest of present facts; something that gives meaning to all that passes, and yet eludes apprehension; something whose possession is the final good, and yet is beyond reach; something which is the ultimate ideal, and yet the hopeless quest.[6]

It is because of the constant dynamic tensions between ought and is, between the eternal vision and present realities, between that which we apprehend and that which apprehends us, that a given religion cannot be reduced to an essence—propositions about the divine and moral maxims —which can then be combined with other essences in order to form an ideal blend.

It is not what may be learned from non-Christian religions which interests me but what may be learned from men who live by them. What I am advocating is not merely that Christians acquire information about Judaism, Islam, Hinduism, Buddhism, etc., but that they imaginatively place themselves within cultural and social situations other than their own. It is interesting to learn how others conceive of the divine, the accomplishment of their founders and leaders, the contents of their confessions and scriptures, the nature of their ceremonies, their understanding of the "good life," and their anticipations regarding human destiny. But religion is much more than the data which fills these categories, Religion is a complete structuring of experience, an integrating of all elements of one's experience. A man's religion is his relationship with that which he regards as permanent or central in the nature of things. And this relationship influences his thoughts, his feelings, his actions, and the society in which he lives. If we skim theological and ethical ideas from the top, we have access only to what a man believes or professes to believe. Beliefs are no more religion than marriage manuals are sexuality; a football rule book is the Super Bowl; or a papier-mâché globe is the world.

The attitude of openness to the faith of other men advocated in these pages should not be confused with the syncretism encouraged by the universalist. Radical displacement and universalism represent two extremes which must be avoided. The attitude of war cuts the Christian off from the human family, diminishes his growth, and destroys his ability to contribute to the solution of mankind's fundamental problems. But the uncritical acceptance of the alien by the universalist and the total misinterpretation of the nature of religion which governs his efforts are no more palatable.

FULFILLMENT

The theory that Christianity fulfills or "crowns" all major religions is immensely popular. This theory claims that Christianity holds the truths of all major religions. According to this view, God has revealed himself in many ways—through the Law and prophets to the Hebrew tribes, through Zoroaster to the Persians, through the ancient rishis or forest seers to the people of India, through the ministry of the Buddha to Asians, etc. God has given a measure of light to all men. In Christ the aspiration of each religion has been fulfilled. Thus, the Gospel is the crown of every religion.

This view is based on the traditional Christian understanding of the relationship of the two covenants or testaments. Jesus taught that he had come not to abrogate the Law or Old Covenant but to fulfill it. Since its earliest days, the Church has considered itself the inheritor of the Covenant, the true or spiritual Israel. (We note in passing that the problem of the peculiar relationship of the two covenant peoples of God, the Jewish people and the Church, has never been particularly well defined.) The advocate of the fulfillment theory sees non-Christian religions as an indirect preparation for the Gospel, which complements the direct preparation of the Hebrew Scriptures (the Christian "Old Testament").

R. C. Zaehner's *The Comparison of Religions* (1962) offers a full account of this view. Zaehner maintains that the teachings of all religions point to, prepare for, and are consummated in Jesus Christ. The following quotations illustrate the fulfillment theorist's attitude:

> Christ indeed comes to fulfill not only the law and the prophets of Israel, but also the "law and prophets" of the Aryan race. He fulfills or rounds out the conception of God independently revealed to the Hebrew prophets and to Zoroaster, and by His Crucifixion, Death, Resurrection,

and Ascension He points to the type of mystical path the soul must tread if it is to rise beyond the *atman* or higher self to its predestined reunion with God.

Christ is the true Bodhisattva, God made Man, suffering with man, and crucified by man and for man that He might release him. . . .

Christ . . . arises again in body and in soul, a whole Man who is also God, thereby fulfilling the hope of Zoroaster. The ideal of divine incarnation was well-known to India. . . . This . . . Indian hope is once again fulfilled in Christ. . . .

Christianity, then, does fulfill both the mystical tradition of India as finally expressed in the Bhagavad-Gita and the Bodhisattva doctrine, and the hopes of Zoroaster, the prophet of ancient Iran. In Christ the two streams meet and are harmonized and reconciled as they are nowhere else. . . .[7]

But the critic of the fulfillment view must ask how Hinduism—to cite but one example—a religion with presuppositions regarding human nature, creation, time, and life after death which differ radically from Western religious doctrine, can be said to be "fulfilled" in Christianity. The crown theorist must adjust both Christianity and non-Christian religion so that they will relate to one another in terms of the theory. In Zaehner's case the results are a suspiciously Eastern Christianity composed from bits and pieces of Christian teachings and snippets of conformable Oriental lore. The context, meaning, and intentions of both Christian and non-Christian are completely ignored. The Hinduism, Buddhism, and Zoroastrianism which are presented as precursors of Christianity are as much abstractions and inventions as the Christianity which they are said to antedate!

The major defect of the crown theory is its inability to regard a religion other than Christianity as a source of genuine insight into man's place in the divine structure of things. In the meeting of world religions, the Christian can teach—he can indicate the fulfillment of all other religions in his—but he cannot learn. It is no wonder that non-Christians have regarded the fulfillment theory as another example of the religious imperialism of Western Christianity.

APPRECIATION

The possibility of a change in Roman Catholic attitude appears in the "Declaration on the Relationship of the Church to Non-Christian Religions," one of the most publicized documents of the Second Vatican Council. Attention was focused on this document by the press, radio, and television because of the alleged "exoneration" of the Jews which it contains. Not only does this misinterpret the document but it overlooks the intention and value of the declaration. Its significance lies in the attitude which the fathers of the Church express toward religions other than their own. They unequivocally reject the "rigorist" understanding of non-Christian religions as "the work of Satan." In the words of the declaration, "The Catholic Church rejects nothing which is true and holy in these religions."[8]

The Council "gives primary consideration in this document to what human beings have in common and to what promotes fellowship among them."[9] Mankind is described as a "single community," and the various religions as searches "for answers to those profound mysteries of human condition which, today even as in olden times, deeply stir the human heart."[10] The Council not only recognizes the presence of that which is "true and holy in these religions" but further exhorts Christians "prudently and lovingly, through dialogue and collaboration with the followers of other religions, and in witness of Christian faith and life, acknowledge, preserve, and promote the spiritual and moral goods found among these men, as well as the values in their society and culture."[11]

This exhortation is remarkable for several reasons. First, the Catholic Church recognizes that God is at work in non-Christian religions as "the light which enlightens every man." Second, the Council approves and encourages dialogue and collaboration with these religions—dialogue neither as a precursor of evangelism nor as an abandonment of the soteriological claims of the Christian faith. Third, the declaration specifically recognizes the spiritual and moral values of the religiously developed culture of the non-Christian world (i.e., Hindu India, Buddhist Southeast

Asia, the Muslim Near East). Thus, for Roman Catholics at least, there exists an official approbation of interreligious dialogue and cooperation based on the acknowledgement of the legitimacy, necessity, and value of other religions.

The "Declaration on the Relationship of the Church to Non-Christian Religions" undercuts theories of radical displacement and encourages Christians to seek creative opportunities for cooperation with non-Christians. The Declaration clearly rejects the "my truth versus your error" attitude of war which has been all too characteristic of Christian response to non-Christian religions. Moreover, the Declaration *implicitly* allows for the possibility that Christianity has something to gain as well as something to contribute in the meeting of world religions, for the Council's recognition of the moral, cultural, and religious truths possessed by other religions strongly suggests that these values may express themselves in ways ignored, repressed, or distorted in the "Christian" West.

Unfortunately the *explicit* tone of the Declaration is paternalistic. The stance of the Council, i.e., Christians taking it upon themselves to preserve and promote someone else's "spiritual and moral goods," is inimical to the goals espoused. The ideological basis for the Declaration is a *"logos"* christology, that is, the conviction that Christ is the *logos* or divine reason of whom all mankind partakes. Anyone who lives by reason (in accordance with moral law as adumbrated in the culture of his society) is in some sense a Christian. The *logos* christology presupposed by the

Council requires two premises: (a) There is no salvation apart from the Church and the Gospel which it proclaims; and (b) The Gospel is present and operative in, through, and despite other religions. As Father Raymond Panikkar observes:

> . . . Christ is present in one form or another in every human being on his religious way to God.[12]

> . . . the good and *bona fide* Hindu is saved by Christ and not by Hinduism, but it is through the sacraments of Hinduism, through the message of morality and good life, through *das Mysterion* [the mystery or sacrament] that comes down to him through Hinduism, that Christ saves the Hindu normally. This amounts to saying that Hinduism has also a place in the universal saving providence of God.[13]

But whatever soteriological role Hinduism plays, it does so not as *Hinduism* but as a channel for the Gospel of Jesus Christ, as crypto-Christianity. In other words, Hinduism (or any other non-Christian religion) is legitimated not by its unique insights into the nature and destiny of man but by its capacity for proclaiming contrary to its intentions an alien message, the Christian Gospel. This view allows for a high degree of Christian tolerance and even respect for world religions, but it hardly inclines the Christian toward the serious consideration of the lessons preserved and conveyed by the faiths of other men.

CONFRONTATION AND ASSIMILATION

On both conscious and unconscious levels there has been a constant assimilation by the Christian church of philosophical concepts, social institutions, ethical teachings, architecture, art, and even religious formulations of non-Christian origin. The ethical monotheism of Zoroastrian Persia left an indelible mark upon Jewish religious thought (and through the Jews upon Christianity). The Christian Church was born within Judaism and owes its earliest scriptures (the Hebrew Bible), sacraments, forms of worship, and community discipline to the Jewish people. The Church Fathers and the framers of the Catholic creeds relied upon the categories and vocabulary of Greek philosophy. The legal structure of Imperial Rome thus became the basis not only for ecclesiastical law but for the formation of the Holy Roman Empire.

The history of Christianity is thus the record of constant interaction between the Gospel and the cultural forms through which the Church expresses its doctrine, celebrates its liturgy, and governs its corporate life. For the Church must either speak to the world in the language of the world or remain silent and irrelevant in the face of human need. Of course, there are perils in relating the eternal Gospel to the temporal circumstances. Institutions have a way of confusing cultural forms of expression with the religious substance which these forms convey. When this occurs both religion and culture suffer. Religion confines itself to the cultural forms of a given time and place, thereby insuring its unintelligibility to later generations. The elevation by religion of the cultural forms of a given period arrests the growth of culture, forcing the artist, the lawmaker, the philosopher, and the architect to preserve the religiously sanctioned norms of the past instead of applying creative insight to the situation of the present.

The ambiguity of religion and culture has encouraged many to seek to separate the kernel of the Gospel from the forms through which it is conveyed. Virtually every reformer in the history of the Church has sought to sort wheat from chaff, the so-called primitive Christian message from the interpretation and application of that message by successive generations. In the second century, Tertullian insisted that there was no point of contact between revelation and philosophy, between the Gospel and human religion. Martin Luther considered the Reformation a return to the Christianity of the New Testament and a rejection of the corruption of that faith by the hierarchical Church of his day. At the beginning of the twentieth century, Adolf Harnack attacked the "hellenization of the Gospel" by the Church Fathers. He claimed that the essential message of Jesus—the proclamation of the coming kingdom; the fatherhood of God; the infinite value of the human soul; and a higher righteousness motivated by love— had been perverted during the patristic period. In their struggles with Hellenistic thought and Gnostic religious tendencies, argued Harnack, the Church Fathers had accommodated the pristine Gospel to the cultural situation of their day and thus corrupted it.

In more recent years much has been written about the alleged pollution of the primal faith of the earliest Christians. Both Catholicism and Protestantism (particularly within the neoorthodox camp) have produced several thinkers who have warned about the dangers of allowing the Gospel to be perverted by alien cultural or religious forms. But such warnings are motivated by an absurd romanticism. For it is impossible to separate the pure Gospel from the contributions of individuals and societies who have received its message, experienced its renewing power, and sought to discover the meaning of all things in the light of the divine Presence. Modern man does not live in the primitive Church. He can never more than approximate the faith, liturgy, and community life of the early Church. And this he does not by rejecting the impact of the present situation but by attempting to live as a Christian in his spatio-temporal world, by seeking to discover the will of God for these circumstances, by striving to bring institutions, structures, and forms of contemporary human existence into dialogue with the Lord of history.

Recent developments in Christian missionary efforts indicate the weaknesses of binding Christianity to unalterable forms. Unless the Church allows for the evolution of indigenous forms of liturgy, polity, social organization, and even doctrinal expression, the Church will wither away in Africa, Asia, the Caribbean, and other parts of the world. The future of the Church universal will be determined in large measure by the ability of Western Christianity to foster and appreciate both a hymnody and theology which bloom in soil other than the Hebrew-Greek-Roman civilization of the West. Not only are indigenous forms of Christianity desirable for their own sake, but it just may be that they will enable Western Christians to put an end to the absolutizing of Western culture and institutions—a tendency which has led contemporary theology into one cul-de-sac after another.

In a sense, the dialogue of world religions has already begun. Our exposure to one another in the "global village" created by the mass media has triggered a revolution in our relations. But the distorting gaze of newspaper, magazine and television coverage presents us with grave misinterpretations as well as new data. The mass media bombard us with the alien, the unique, the unprecedented. But all too often they offer shadows instead of substance, fleeting images instead of reality. At the same time, the news media reveal the inner inconsistencies and failures of our "business as usual" way of life. The result is that we are confused and frightened by the new but no longer comfortable with the platitudes, maxims, values, and commonplaces of the past.

The time is ripe for a rethinking of personal values,

religious convictions, ethical standards, and social responsibilities. In the following chapters we shall look at the dilemmas of modern life through the eyes of the Hindu, the Buddhist, the Jew, and the modern "secular religionist." We shall presuppose neither the superiority nor the inferiority of these ways of life alien to our own. But from the outset we acknowledge the sincerity and integrity of the non-Christian's commitment as well as the dignity of his efforts to actualize the ideals of his traditions. We shall be as patient with his failures to realize the high aims of his religion as we are with our own inability to fulfill the stringent demands of the Sermon on the Mount. We shall honor and respect his achievements as we would have him esteem ours. With an open mind, with an eagerness to learn, with a willingness to accept what is valid and to reject what is untenable, we shall approach Hinduism, Buddhism, Judaism and contemporary religious surrogates as the dynamic faiths of real men. We shall seek neither to convince nor to convert but to appreciate the basic commitments which govern the growth of individuals and the development of living communities.

NOTES

[1] Joel Fort, quoted in Joseph Adcock, "The Marijuana Mess," *Sunday Bulletin Magazine*, Philadelphia (January 12, 1969), p. 10.

[2] "Buddhism and Christianity as a Problem of Today," *Japanese Religions* (Kyoto, Japan) III, 2 (Summer 1963), p. 14.

[3] Review of The Bridge: A Yearbook of Judaeo-Christian Studies in Judaism, IV (Summer 1963).

[4] Ninian Smart, A Dialogue of Religions (London: SCM Press, 1960), p. 130.

[5] H. van Straelin, The Catholic Attitude Toward Other Religions (Westminster, Md.: Newman Press, 1966). For this and similar expressions of "rigorism," see pp. 1–20.

[6] Alfred North Whitehead, Science and the Modern World (New York: Macmillan Company, 1925), pp. 267–268.

[7] R. C. Zaehner, The Comparison of Religions (Boston: Beacon Press, 1962), p. 180. Originally published as At Sundry Times: An Essay in the Comparison of Religions (London: Faber and Faber, Ltd.).

[8] Op. cit., The Documents of Vatican II (New York: Guild Press, America Press, and Association Press, 1966), p. 662.

[9] Ibid., p. 660.

[10] Ibid., p. 661.

[11] Ibid., pp. 662–663.

[12] Raymond Panikkar, "Hinduism and Christianity," Religion and Society (Bangalore, India), December 1961, p. 11.

[13] Ibid., p. 17.

2

<<<<<<<<<<<<<<<<<<<<<<<<<<<<<<<<<<<<<<<<<<<<<<<

The Hindu Attitude toward
Other Religions

Into the bosom of the one great sea
Flow streams that come from hills on every side.
Their names are various as their springs,
And thus in every land do men bow down
To one great God, though known by many names.
— A South Indian Folksong

THE MESSAGE OF VIVEKANANDA

IT WAS A CHILLY summer evening in Chicago. Narenda
Nath Datta was lost, cold, tired, and alone. The thirty-
year old Indian was in a strange country. He was completely
unfamiliar with its customs and its people. He wandered
the streets making inquiries, but he had blundered into the
German quarter and no one could understand him. Finally

he found an empty crate in the corner of a railroad station. He climbed in and there slept the night.

The next morning he arose early and began begging food from door to door, only to discover, as door after door was slammed in his face, that Chicago is not India.

Later the same day, September 11, 1893, he took his seat as Swami Vivekananda, Hindu delegate to the World's Parliament of Religions (held in conjunction with the Columbian Exposition which attracted my grandfather to Chicago). He was introduced during the afternoon session, and stepped forward to speak. He began, "Sisters and Brothers of America." The huge audience reacted to his warmth immediately. For two full minutes they cheered and applauded the young swami. When order was restored he spoke for about four minutes, yet his short speech became the keynote address of the parliament and the announcement to the world of the Hindu attitude toward all religions. "We believe not only in universal toleration," he said, "but we accept all religions as true."

Swami Vivekananda was destined to live only nine more years—but in those years he became the first to interpret the treasures of Indian religion and culture as a living, dynamic force to the West, and by his success in the Occident turned the hearts of millions of Hindus to their own neglected heritage. In hundreds of lectures delivered in the United States, Britain, and on the European continent, Vivekananda expounded Hindu spirituality. The following lecture which I have reconstructed from his collected writings and from the reports of his followers is typical of his message:

> Nothing has brought to man more blessings than religion, yet at the same time there is nothing that has brought more horror. Religion is the highest plane of human thought and life. The intensest love that humanity has ever known has come from religion, and the most diabolical hatred. Nothing makes us so cruel as religion, and nothing makes us so tender.
>
> All men are involved in the search for God, for this is the search for human destiny. Even as our social struggles are represented by various social organizations, so is man's spiritual struggle represented by various religions.
>
> As we examine the various great religions we discover that there is a tremendous life-power in all. Every sect has a meaning, a great idea, imbedded within itself. Both common sense and history teach that each should be allowed to live. Further, no great world religion has ever died, each of them is actually progressing and growing.
>
> The diversity of religions is required by the absolute individuality of each man. I am glad that sects exist, and I only wish they may go on multiplying more and more, for without the constant clash of differing thoughts, thinking would come to an end. Now, if we all thought alike, we would be like Egyptian mummies in a museum looking vacantly at one another's faces;—no more than that! It is this difference, this losing of balance between us, which is the very soul of our progress, the soul of all our thoughts. Sects must be allowed to multiply until at last there will

be as many sects as human beings, and each one will have his own method, his individual method of thought in religion.

But how can such a variety of religions be true? If one thing is true must not its negation be false? I do not see religions as contradictory at all, but as supplementary. Each religion takes up one part of the great universal truth, and spends its whole force in embodying and typifying that part of the great truth. The religious panorama reveals the march of humanity from truth to truth— from lesser to higher—rather than from error to truth. All these religions are different forces in the economy of God, working for the good of mankind; and not one can become dead, not one can be killed.

Moreover it is useless to speculate about the realization of the "universal religion." It already exists. If the priests and other people who have taken upon themselves the task of preaching different religions simply cease preaching for a few moments, we shall see it is there. It exists in the growing number of sects, and the greater the number the more chance of people getting religion. I have personally urged American Mormons to introduce their religion into India. A man's religion must speak his own language, the language of his own soul. The fuller the menu, the more likely it is that one will be satisfied.

The attitude of the religious man as he views this diversity is neither exclusivistic arrogance which claims to possess the whole truth, nor liberal tolerance. Toleration is blasphemy. I believe in acceptance. I shall go into the mosque of the Muslim; I shall enter the Christian's church and kneel; I shall enter the Buddhist temple, where

I shall take refuge in the Buddha and in his law. I shall go into the forest and sit down in meditation with the Hindu, who is trying to see the Light which enlightens the heart of every one.

I shall not destroy. I shall not injure. In my mission to the nations, I shall not say a word against any man's convictions. I seek to take a man where he stands and from thence give him a lift. For all that a teacher can do is remove the obstructions a little so that a man may find his own path to union with the divine.[1]

Vivekananda's encouragement of religious diversity and his acceptance of the validity of religions other than his own must not blind us to the conservative side of his thought. There are many religions according to the different needs, circumstances, and capabilities of various groups of men. But the ultimate standard by which all religions are measured—the goal to which they lead—is Vedanta, the classic Hinduism espoused by Vivekananda and conveyed by the monastic order of teachers which he organized to carry on his work.

THE HINDU ATTITUDE
TOWARD OTHER RELIGIONS

A majority of educated Hindus would agree with Vivekananda that the various religions are not incompatibles but complementaries. In the words of Sarvepalli Radhakrishnan, the former President of India, "Let us believe in a unity of spirit and not of organization, a unity which secures ample liberty not only for every individual but for every type of organized life which has proven itself effective."[2] At the same time, Radhakrishnan insists that Vedantic Hinduism is the norm by which other religions are judged. For Radhakrishnan as for Vivekananda, a religion is valid in the degree to which it approximates Vedantic truth. This does not mean that Hinduism expects other religions to conform to its structure of belief and worship.

Hinduism rejects the notion that religion is the acceptance of theological abstraction or the observance of ceremonies. Religion is an insight into the nature of reality and the entrance of the whole man into nature by means of that insight. Religious experience is self-certifying. Nevertheless the religious man cannot retreat into the security of his inner assurance. As a man living in the world of men, he is compelled to justify his inner convictions in order to satisfy the demands of his own rationality and the critical standards of his fellows. Religious experience is not a rare moment of intense bliss but a breaking through the surface of reality to the depths of being. Once he has penetrated the veil of everyday illusion, a man cannot be as he was before. Every thought, every activity, every responsibility is seen in a new light.

Every society regards—indeed must regard—its own religious heritage as sacred in order to insure its own continuity. However, Hinduism tempers its loyalty to its own tradition with the recognition that revelation is never completed or final. Radhakrishnan declares that Christian theology has made itself irrelevant to all but those "who share or accept a particular kind of spiritual experience." But the Hindu understanding of God's love for all men requires that the Hindu readily admit points of view other than his own. In diverse ways, different men and communities have sought and attained the self-transforming union with the divine. Each insight deserves to be respected. Each has a place in the history of man's quest after God-realization.

The Hindu views even his own religion as a critical, progressive unification of varied intuitions of reality, for Hinduism is a subtly unified mass of mythologies, ascetic disciplines, and theological speculations. The history of Hinduism is the chronicle of continual experimentation with new forms to produce new ideals to suit new conditions. And yet at each stage there is both development and basic continuity—an interplay of new circumstances with the Vedanta, the timeless essence of Hinduism. The term "Vedanta" literally means the "end (concluding portions) of the Vedas," ancient scriptures dealing with cultic practice. As used by Hindu writers, *Vedanta* refers to the systems of speculative religious thought which developed as a result of centuries of interpretation of the Vedas. Over several centuries the intimate teachings of ancient rishis or seers were collected. This literature, usually in the form of dialogues between master and disciple, is known as the

Upanishads (literally, "to sit near"). The Upanishads do not directly interpret the Vedas but expound the insights regarding nature, man, and God which are implicit both in the Vedas and the everyday religion of India.

The Upanishads center around the Brahman Atman doctrine. According to this fundamental conviction, the universal Spirit (*Brahman*) and the true Self of each individual (*Atman*) are identical. A man's true Self is an expression or manifestation of the divine Spirit. In the Chandogya Upanishad, this identity is expressed in the formula which is at the core of all Hindu religious thought: "*Tat tvam asi*" (That art thou). When a man, through the fulfillment of all duties, the discipline of all physical functions, and the control of all mental faculties, penetrates to the very center or ground of his being, he discovers the one really existent entity, the all-inclusive, unitary Being.

Of nearly equal importance in the thought of the Upanishadic seers is the "neti-neti" (neither this nor that) doctrine. In the words of the Kena Upanishad, "He truly knows Brahman who knows him as beyond knowledge; he who thinks he knows, knows not." Given any set of alternatives, Brahman is *neither*, and yet, *both*. For even though the unitary ground of all things is present at the very core of each, it infinitely transcends them. According to the Upanishads, Brahman is above all distinctions. Yet, says the Brihadaranyaka Upanishad, the divine has assumed all forms in order to reveal itself in all forms. The divine cannot be poured into a single conceptual mold. Its infinite richness demands a humility on the part of the adherent of any religion as well as a recognition that his grasp of the absolute Spirit is but a partial one.

Although all Vedantist thinkers agree on the essential doctrines expressed in the *tat tvam asi* and *neti-neti* formulae, there are rival schools. The *Vedanta Sutra*, reputedly the work of Badarayana, a teacher of the first century B.C., was the first attempt to systematize the teachings of the Upanishads. The different systems of Vedantic philosophy are the result of attempts to interpret these difficult aphorisms. *Sankara* (eighth century A.D.), the most famous exponent of Vedanta, was responsible for *advaita* (nondualistic) Vedanta. This school holds that the world has no reality independent of Brahman. The impersonal, incomprehensible Brahman alone exists. All else is *maya* or illusion. The liberation of man comes when he conquers the illusion that his *atman* or true self has any reality apart from Brahman.

Later Vedantists, *Ramanuja* and *Madhva*, were prominent representatives of the school of Vedanta known as *dvaita* (dualistic). Ramanuja (eleventh century A.D.) claimed that the world, the human soul, and God are distinct though not separate. The physical world and individual souls make up the "body" of the Supreme Being, the Lord Vishnu. Vishnu is the inner controller leading all souls to liberation. Madhva, author of the third form of Vedanta, lived in the thirteenth century, and was no doubt influenced by Islam and Christianity. According to his teaching, the dualism between Brahman and individual souls is absolute. The goal of man's spiritual quest is eternal bliss in the presence of Vishnu. The Lord Vishnu is the highest reality, but the world is also real. Eternal bliss in the presence of Vishnu awaits those who offer him *bhakti* (faithful devotion).

The philosophically inclined Hindu tends to regard the dualistic Vedanta of Madhva and the modified nondualism of Ramanuja as dialectical steps leading to the full truth of nondualistic or *advaita* Vedanta. The nondualist views the awesome Lord worshipped by the followers of Ramanuja and Madhva as one of the many forms which the impersonal, all-encompassing Brahman assumes in relation to mankind. The theism of these schools, argues the *advaita* Vedantist, is not wrong but only preliminary. The monistic teachings of the Upanishads as interpreted by Sankara are not a religion, "but religion itself in its most universal and deepest significance."

But how does the Hindu account for the divisive disagreements of religion? And how is Hinduism able to harmonize its commitment to the immutable truths of Vedanta with the existence of religions which are not based on these truths? In essence, Hinduism deals with these problems by calling attention to the necessary *relativism* and *agnosticism* of all true religion. The Hindu insists:

Religious experience is not the pure unvarnished presentment of the real in itself, but the presentment of the real already influenced by the ideas and prepossessions of the perceiving mind. . . . Each religious genius spells out the mystery of God according to his own endowment, personal, racial, and historical. The variety of pictures of God is easily intelligible when we realize that religious experience is psychologically mediated.[3]

Because God is hidden, all descriptions of him fall short of their mark, disclosing more about the *subject* who utters them than about the *object* of worship and devotion. Every religion must admit the ultimate impenetrability of the divine. Because our understanding of the religious mystery is determined by our prepossessions, there is a variety of pictures, each of which arises from encounter with the divine, but none of which completely overcomes the subjectivity of the individual consciousness in which it arises.

But no matter how sound such agnosticism may be as an expression of the mystery confronted, it is utterly unsatisfying to the everyday needs of man. In daily experience, the hidden must yield to the vision of the religious imagination. And since the category of personality is the highest that man can conceive, he imagines the transcendent Brahman in personal terms. Although Hinduism recognizes the religious value of theistic or personal concepts of God, it strictly maintains the suprapersonal character of the universal Spirit. As Radhakrishnan relates: "When we emphasize the nature of reality in itself we get the absolute Brahman; when we emphasize its relation to us we get the personal Bhagavan (Lord)."[4] Hinduism does not reject any idea of God, but values them according to a hierarchy of value. As man's spiritual life develops he moves from fear of natural forces to veneration of sages; to devotion for such divine "incarnations" as Rama, Krishna, and the Buddha; to worship of the personal God; and, finally, to the beatific union with the impersonal Brahman.

The Hindu distinguishes ideas of God not as true and false but as more or less adequate to the Vedantic standards. No expression of the religious life is rejected as utterly erroneous, for the inexhaustibility of the divine nature requires an infinite number of manifestations—all of which are true, but none of which is complete. All representations of the divine are relative, preliminary, and symbolic. Because of this ideological humility, Hinduism has been remarkably free of both heresy-hunting and the strange obsession of Western religions that acceptance of a particular intellectual representation of the divine is necessary for salvation. In addition, the Hindu recognition of the universality of divine self-revelation encourages an openness to the alien and a willingness to learn from it. Thus, Hindu interaction with other religions has been marked by a constant but critical incorporation of the new. The historic instances are legion: the transformation of primitive Vedism into classical Hinduism; the absorption of the teaching of the Buddha; the reform movements of Ramanada, Caitanya, and Kabir which grew out of the Hindu confrontation with Islam; the iconoclastic social reform movements which arose in response to Western culture and religion during the British occupation.

At the same time, Hinduism has sought to give as well as receive. While admitting that the various religions are not contradictory but rather supplementary, Hinduism has demanded that each live up to its profoundest insights. It sees itself charged with a mission to the nations—the mission of removing obstacles so that each man may find union with the divine through the religion of his own social and cultural environment. Hinduism has been eager to share its own rich religious heritage with the nations—not in hope of converting others to Hinduism but in order to call attention to the one truth which is hidden in the depths of all religions. The Hindu is willing to teach the Christian, the Jew, the Buddhist, the Muslim, or the religiously uprooted. But he is careful neither to molest nor condemn and to remain open to the spiritual discoveries of others.

THE LIMITS OF HINDU TOLERANCE

Hinduism represents a critical acceptance of other religions. The Hindu believes that he is able to gain something from his exposure to alien traditions. But his attitude is governed by principles which require that he must inevitably refute and reject some elements of any religion, while accepting and absorbing other aspects. The negative aspect of the Hindu attitude toward other religions may be illustrated by reference to the criticism made of Christianity by Hindu spokesmen.

Hindu criticism of Christianity may be classified under two headings: (1) Objections to Christian doctrine; (2) Objections to Christian missions. Obviously the distinction is not absolute. The primary Hindu objection is to the exclusivism of the Christian faith. Not only do Christians immodestly claim that their religion is the only path to God, but they also insist that their incarnation of God is his sole, final, and complete manifestation. Hinduism must strongly deny both assertions. The Hindu views all religions as valid paths to the ultimate summit, as provisional attempts to grasp that which infinitely transcends all conceptualizations. Likewise, the Hindu is accustomed to venerating many incarnations, each of which is regarded as a unique expression of the divine glory. The Christian attitude reveals spiritual arrogance as well as a narrow view of God.

The Hindu also finds himself in fundamental disagreement with the Christian on the whole orbit of theological questions revolving about the question of the nature and needs of man. The Christian sees man as infected by original sin and in need of redemption. There is an urgency to this, for time is short and there is but one life. But the Hindu sees no end to time. Reality never ceases. There is endless opportunity. The individual is fated to be reborn until he rises above the shackles of ignorance and egocentrism. Also the divine is repeatedly present in human experience in the form of an avatar to guide man out of darkness. (Many Indians venerate Gandhi as an avatar.) Thus the urgency of the Christian's one-life-one-savior religion is undercut.

We have mentioned that Hinduism and Christianity differ radically on the nature of the human predicament. Both religions agree that God enters into our humanity to rescue us. According to Christianity, man is in need of redemption from the consequences of his willful opposition to the purposes of God. But the Hindu sees mankind beset by error rather than *sin*. And error is an inadequate interpretation of truth. Only by passing through relatively adequate truths to a full liberation from the fundamental error that the separate ego is of paramount importance can salvation be attained. Thus, the Christian calls upon men to repent and be converted. The Hindu seeks freedom from his egocentric life so that he may find oneness with the divine ground of all beings.

In addition, Christianity and Hinduism hold different views of reality. The Christian view is anthropocentric. Man is viewed as the crown of God's creative activity. The Incarnation is for the restoration of man. The Hindu view is cosmocentric. The divine is the primordial cause of the universe, its all-embracing consciousness. The Hindu seeks not a personal salvation from the world but a reunification with the source of all things, a return to the primal harmony of the universe.

In consequence of their differing views of reality, there is a wide discrepancy between Hindu and Christian attitudes toward nature. The anthropocentrism of the Christian, his conviction that the world was made for his benefit, leads him to exploit the resources of the natural realm with little thought of the consequences for the future. But the Hindu acknowledges his dependence upon a natural order of which he is a part. For this reason, he venerates the cow in order to suppress his sense of total dependence upon the sustaining power of nature. When Sir Edmund Hillary reached the pinnacle of Mount Everest, the Western news media heralded "the conquest of Mount Everest." The Hindu responded quite differently. He felt that Mount Everest had been befriended! After all, the awesome titan of the Himalayas was in no way humbled because a white Anglo-Saxon had set his feet on its summit. Was the grandeur of Everest in any way diminished? Were its terrible, capricious powers in any way subjugated? Hillary may have conquered himself in pursuing his goal—but what arrogance to speak of his accomplishment as "the conquest of Mount Everest!"

Hindu attitudes toward man and nature are alien to traditional Christianity with its strong emphasis on the ultimate gap between man and all other creatures as well as the distance between man and his creator—a gap which not even the most strenuous effort can bridge. However, Western theology has always included a subdominant stream of mystics whose thought is not unlike the Hindu consciousness. Many of the mystics have spoken of a transcendent unity of all beings, of an all-embracing One present in every man as the very core of his existence. The cosmic evolutionary theology of Pierre Teilhard de Chardin provides a recent example. Although Teilhard and Hinduism start from diverse presuppositions, both regard the universe as an evolutionary process guided by the divine Spirit toward the perfection of the individual in a final, all-encompassing unity. According to Teilhard's Christocentric world view, Christ is the reflection, paradigm, and mediator of the evolutionary process. Through Him individual lives are able to attain personal fulfillment as a community of men progressively unfolds, binding man to man through self-transcending love.

But a God whose consciousness and perfection depends upon the spiritual perfection of man is inconsistent with the immutable deity of orthodox theology. It is not surprising that Teilhard bore the suspicions and condemnations which have been the fate of so many mystical theologians. Ironically, the Hindu is able to appreciate Teilhard, the Christian Platonists of Alexandria, Meister Eckhart, Jakob Boehme, and Paul Tillich in a way forbidden to the Christian by the guardians of religious orthodoxy.

Christian orthodoxy inclines man to regard separation as the basic ontological fact. There is an essential distance between man and nature, man and his fellows, man and God. Since the individual consciousness is meeting place of all realms of experience, the mirror of reality, it must be expected that inner divisions and alienations will result.

The experience of each man must reproduce the basic situation of the self set *against* other beings, the environment, and God. Out of his sense of estrangement and threat, the individual has no choice but to respond in a manipulative, exploitative manner. The egocentricity which demands individual fulfillment at the cost of nature and other selves comes to dominate every relationship—personal, social, commercial, and political.

The Western attitude toward nature is the basis of our impressive technological and economic development. Because nature is experienced as essentially dead and alien to man, it may readily be exploited for man's sake. The Hindu desperately craves the material fruits of technology. But he finds that Western science and industry require the acceptance of fundamental assumptions which are foreign to Hinduism. Professor A. K. Saran of Lucknow University, India, explains: "Man and nature are thought of—and invariably experienced—as an organic unity, as integral parts of a cosmos. Man lives in nature and nature lives in man. To a Hindu nature is alive, it bears the signatures of the divine. . . ."[5] For the Hindu, each natural phenomenon is a symbol of the divine ground of all beings. The divine is present in all things, revealing its power through the distinctness of each. Hence the Hindu rejects the distinction between sacred and profane. The entire universe is sacramental. In every experience man may realize his essential oneness with the divine, a unity which embraces nature.

The cosmos is the focus of redemption. By participating in nature, man shares in the reconciling power of the Spirit. Thus, technology appears to the Hindu consciousness as a disintegrating force which sets man against nature, against the divine task of perfecting the natural for its final fulfillment. Gandhi's awareness of the incompatibility of the Western utilitarian attitude toward nature and the Hindu sense of underlying unity led him to oppose the industrialization of India. Saran comments:

> It is a measure of India's failure to develop any modernistic movement from within that Mahatma Gandhi, while actively campaigning for many radical social reforms, at the same time, could stand vehemently and uncompromisingly against all economic development in the Western sense of the term. The Gandhian economy was closed and primitive. During the British rule, not only the Imperial policy, but also Gandhi and the Khadi ideology of the Congress were hostile to India's industrialization. Gandhi's famous boycott movement was directed not only against English and foreign goods, it was equally against Indian factory products.[6]

But, alas, Gandhi's dependence upon the spinning wheel and cottage industry is no solution to the problems which confront India. Only the mechanization of agriculture, the development of modern systems of communication and transportation, the growth of heavy industry, and the application of technical skills can provide India with the material basis for economic stability and national survival. The cruel dilemma is that industrialization (as well as the attendant phenomenon—urbanization) depends on metaphysical assumptions which by their very nature are destructive of the traditional Hindu presuppositions. Whether Hinduism will find direction from the past for the quandaries of today or whether it will be supplanted by a utilitarian pragmatism, as the traditional religions of China have been by dialectical materialism, remains to be seen.

Where there is honest discussion between Hindu and Christian, such issues will be matters of contention. For the Hindu's openness to other religions does not silence his opposition to what he regards as fundamental delusions and errors. Yet, since he knows that even his own conceptualizations of ultimate reality are only tentative and provisional, he will temper his criticism with humility. However, there is one matter which forces him to voice his opinion with fervor and persistence—the question of Christian missions to India.

The Hindu objects to Christian missionary activity for two main reasons: (1) Christian missions undermine the cultural-social foundations of Indian life, and (2) the missionary enterprise, though lofty in purpose, is going about its business in the wrong way.

As the Hindu sees it, the chief fruit of Christian missions to India is dissension. By their constant disparagement of a culture which they have seldom bothered to study, the missionaries have produced a nationwide inferiority complex. Further, they have taught their converts to hate their heritage and their people (if not themselves as well). The missionaries have set son against father, brother against brother, wife against husband.

Rightly or wrongly, the Hindu also condemns Christianity for having been a tool of European imperialism during the period of colonization. As an Indian Christian, J. J. Kumarappa, observed forty years ago: "the East has come to think of Christianity as part of the political game of the West. In religion it talks of 'going about doing good': in politics this takes the form of 'ruling others for their good.' . . . Before the Christians went to Africa the Africans had lands but no Bibles; now they have Bibles but no lands."[7]

The second objection is even more telling. If the Christian missionaries are trying to enrich the spiritual life of the average Indian, they are doing a poor job of it and had better turn to their more experienced brethren for assistance. To begin with, the missionaries have an extremely faulty notion of why they are in India. They desire, as do all truly religious men, to share their spiritual insights and blessings with others. And this desire no Hindu can condemn. However, the missionaries think that the way to do this is to convert Indians. They attempt to convince the Hindu of his sinfulness, of his participation in the fall of Adam. They expect that a personal crisis, and an intense inner transformation will follow. But the Hindu distrusts the sudden crisis conversions which he has witnessed. He agrees with the Christian missionary that there is need for commitment, self-surrender, and renewal. But he insists that the desirable experience is a gradual, disciplined overcoming of ignorance and its consequences rather than an overwhelming emotional transformation.

The Hindu cannot understand why the Christian preacher does not seem to be conscious of the necessity of spiritual practices. The missionary thinks that when a person has gone through a ritualistic conversion his religious life is satisfied. But Hinduism insists upon discipline. Otherwise the personality of the convert is left to disintegrate under the impact of daily experience.

Surely, contend Hindu thinkers, no one knows more about the discipline of the spiritual life than those who have labored countless centuries to understand the godward aspirations of the human spirit. As Swami Akhilananda insists: "Let the missionary come to the Hindu and learn. Let the missionary save his own soul first, thoroughly establishing himself in God consciousness by purifying and unifying his own emotions." Then, with lips sealed, let him go forth and win converts. Gandhi advised the Christian: "Don't talk about Christianity. The rose doesn't have to propagate its perfume. It just gives it forth, and people are drawn to it. Don't talk about it. Live it. And people will come to see the source of your power."

CONCLUSIONS

Our survey of the attitude of contemporary Hinduism toward other religions is far from exhaustive. Although the view we have examined is the normative Hindu view, it is by no means the only Hindu view. Hinduism is never quite so simple. Like all religions, Hinduism has its rigorists, who demand the suppression of all other religions. One of India's political parties, the RSS (Rastrya Swayamseval Sangha) crusades for the establishment of a Hindu state. Proponents of such a view include the members of the Arya Samaj, an organization which clings to the infallibility of the Vedas, seeks the extirpation of all foreign religions, and which devotes itself to incessant propaganda and social service through such agencies as the Arya Tract Society, the Young Men's Arya Association, and the Vedic Salvation Army! Despite its extreme negativity, its religious obscurantism, and its obvious imitation of Christian missionary methods, the Arya Samaj's record of philanthropic achievement is remarkable. Also we must not overlook the contributions of others, such as Nobel laureate Rabindranath Tagore, whose thought has developed in ways quite distinct from the liberalism of normative Hinduism.

However, it can hardly be questioned that widespread throughout India are views of sympathetic though critical regard for other religions. Radhakrishnan's attitude of cautious absorption without any commitment to missionary activity is probably representative of Hindu intellectuals. Among the common people a benign, often indifferent tolerance prevails. Certainly the violent antiwesternism of the Arya Samaj and the RSS is not widely encouraged nor, for that matter, is the aggressive missionary Vedantism of the Ramakrishnan Order. The ordinary Hindu does not expect that absorption and assimilation are destined to continue until there is one universal religion, but rather that men, in ways as varied as themselves, will realize their divinity. In the end only the quest is one.

We have seen that contemporary Hindu thinkers are willing to confront other religions on the basis of (1) their conviction that Hinduism is able to reconceptualize itself and benefit from religious dialogue and cooperation; and (2) the expectation that other religions have something to gain from exposure to Vedantic spirituality. These presuppositions grow out of the fundamental Hindu concepts of *neti-neti* and *tat-tvam-asi*. For the *neti-neti*, the recognition of the utter incomprehensibility of God forces the Hindu to question even his most cherished formulations of the truth, and, as the history of Hinduism illustrates, to remain open to new insights. The *tat-tvam-asi* doctrine, the conviction that God is present in every human life as the very essence of being, requires that the Hindu listen attentively to what others have discovered in the depths of their innermost selves.

As Paul Tillich observed in *Christianity and the Encounter of the World Religions*, it would be a tremendous step forward if Christians would adopt a similar attitude toward other religions. For implicit in any dialogue between two men is the silent discussion within each participant through which one's own convictions are judged and deepened. As a careful examination of the history of Christianity reveals, Christian faith does not require (and has certainly not benefited from) the out-of-hand rejection of other religions. From the time of the early church's confrontation with Judaism and Hellenism until the present, Christian thought has experienced continual cross-fertilization. When one approaches a foreign reality as a prey to be captured, creative synthesis is excluded. But when one approaches another man's religion on the basis of the common human nature which all men share and the one God who enlightens every man, both that man and his religion cease to be foreign. And when they are no longer alien, other religions drive us to the limits of our self-understanding. For knowledge of only one manifestation of the Spirit may turn out to be knowledge of none. As the sages, seers, and spiritually wise of all religions realize, there is no creativity except on the boundaries to which the inner tensions of faith and the external pressures of the hitherto unknown force us.

NOTES

[1] Selected from *The Complete Works of Swami Vivekananda* (Mayavati, Almora, Himalayas, 1922), Vol. II, p. 358.

[2] S. Radhakrishnan, *The Hindu View of Life* (New York: Macmillan, 1927), p. 58.

[3] *Ibid.*, p. 25.

[4] *Ibid.*, p. 31.

[5] "Hinduism and Economic Development in India," *The Impact of Modern Culture on Traditional Religions* (Leiden: E. J. Brill, 1968), I, p. 128 (Proceedings of the XIth International Congress of the International Association for the History of Religions).

[6] *Ibid.*, p. 130.

[7] Harper's Magazine (April 1927), pp. 599–600.

‹‹‹‹‹‹‹‹‹‹‹‹

MYSTICISM
AND
MODERN MAN

3

<<<<<<<<<<<<<<<<<<<<<<<<<<<<<<<<<<<<<<<<<<<<<

The Religion of the Hippies

HIPPIEDOM IS DEAD. Hounded by the authorities, terrorized by thugs, victimized by the unscrupulous, disoriented by the drug-induced ecstasy through which they sought the shattering and reintegrating intensity characteristic of all genuine religious experience—the "love generation" melted away. Unrestrained hedonists, aimless drifters, and violently resentful young adults have replaced the gentle and religious. The newcomers dress like Hippies, use the same drugs, employ the Hippie argot, live in the same hovels. But the two groups are as different as the words "ignore" and "flaunt." The Hippies ignored adult society. Those who came in their wake flaunt their nonconformity to incense that same society.

What produced the Hippies? What were they seeking? What did they discover? What is their future? What can we learn from them? These are the unavoidable quandaries posed by the ephemeral but significant age of the Hippies. In this chapter, I would like to approach the Hippies as a religious phenomenon. Of course, they were much more and much less. Many of the love generation responded totally to a psychedelically experienced ultimate reality which profoundly transformed their lives and which bound them together in complex communities characterized by immense vitality and cultural creativity. It is this dimension of their experience which most interests the present writer. I am not claiming that every psychedelic experience was a religious experience, any more than my every visit to a Christian church is for me a religious experience. But if we accept such criteria for religious experience as those proposed by Joachim Wach, we can readily see that the psychedelic experience possesses the necessary qualifications. First, the psychedelic experience is described by those who have undergone it as an experience of ultimate reality. Second, it is *a total response of the total being.* Third, the *intensity* of the experience is beyond doubt. Fourth, the psychedelic experience *issues in action,* culminating in a distinct way of life.

WHAT PRODUCED THEM?

The Hippie and his religion cannot be understood apart from the society which unwillingly produced them. If we may adopt Marshall McLuhan's characterization, the Hippie is the child of the tension between the alphabetic and electronic epochs. Before the invention of printing, man lived in a world of acoustic space. The ear experiences reality as boundless, threatening, inescapable, and completely intermingled. Since the Renaissance and the introduction of the portable, privately owned book, man has lived in visual space. The eye attends to one discrete phenomenon at a time. The world is alphabetically apprehended as if it consisted of logically separable, constituent parts. The visual mentality divides reality into distinguishable, independent observers set against objective data which may be known, analyzed, and controlled. Visuality has given birth to technology, science, and individualism—fostering objectivity and detachment (the single reader or observer as the center of his own universe) at the cost of personal involvement and interpersonal participation. Visuality engenders continuous specialization and depersonalization, destroying man's native ability to perceive the all-togetherness of reality.

At present, we are in process of changing the medium through which we perceive the world and through which our environment works us over (one meaning of McLuhan's multifarious pun, "the medium is the massage"). We are entering the age of electronic circuitry—omnipresent radio, all-seeing television, distance-destroying telephone, omniscient data processors. The new medium is much more involved than the former one. It replaces reliance upon the eye and its print technology with the total use of all the senses and the participation of man in his environment.

Today's youth both long for and belong to the emerging,

all-involving world. The late Robert F. Kennedy spoke of the present younger generation as follows: "Not since the founding of the Republic . . . has there been a younger generation of Americans brighter, better educated, more highly motivated than this one. . . . This generation of young people has shown an idealism and a devotion to country matched in few nations, and excelled in none." In his inaugural address, President Richard M. Nixon echoed this sentiment: "We see the hope of tomorrow in the youth of today. I know America's youth. I believe in them. We can be proud that they are better educated, more committed, more passionately driven by conscience than any generation in our history."

If McLuhan's analysis is correct (and I believe that it is), the thousands of hours of immersion in the world via television and the other mass media are a major reason for the passionate involvement which Senator Kennedy and President Nixon praise. But are the Kennedys and Nixons aware of the generational conflict which this exposure has spawned? As Lewis S. Feuer contends, the relations between the young and their elders are normally stable, albeit tense. However, generational stability can be upset by a major social or political failure which "de-authoritizes" them in the eyes of their sons.[1] Robert Paul Wolff, professor of philosophy at Columbia University, grants that the American student's natural belief in the authority of his elders has been severely shaken. But he claims that the reason is neither social or political. He argues:

America has lost no wars; it has suffered no depressions. The generation of the fathers has achieved an unbroken chain of material successes for almost 30 years. If the failure is neither *military* nor *economic*, we can only conclude that it is essentially *moral*. Listen to the voices of the students. They accuse the fathers of the very crimes that the fathers lay at the door of Nazi Germany and Communist Russia: racism, genocide, imperialism, aggression, authoritarian manipulation of subject populations for selfish and evil ends.[2]

Our contemporaries fall into two categories: those who can eat during the evening news and those who dare not try. The Hippie was the squeamish child of iron-stomached parents. His simplicity and naiveté were reactions to the selfish materialism of his middle class parents. His weak stomach could not endure comfortable indifference to the needs of the common family created by the mass media. The Hippie participated in the six o'clock news; his parents in the commercials.

WHAT WERE THEY SEEKING?

The Hippie fled the total externality of the life which his elders offered him. Most of his peers did not flee with him. For they are content with a so-called liberal education which forces a stream of unrelated facts through their consciousness, numbing the neophyte and forever arresting his ability to discover patterns of coherence and meaning. They are content to govern their lives according to the dictates of a vulgar, unprincipled capitalism which depends upon the stable family to consume the shoddy and the unnecessary. But the Hippie was troubled by the hollow vapidity, the insensitivity, the hypocrisy, the downright inhumanity of modern mass culture.

The Hippie dropped out of straight society because of his utter pessimism, his inability to find meaning in middle class existence. He saw his parents' lives as an endless cycle of absurdities and banal responses. The Hippie protest against such entrapment found eloquent expression in the folk laureates: Bob Dylan, Paul Simon (of Simon and Garfunkle), Phil Ochs, and the Beatles' Lennon and McCartney. The horrible fear of being forced to relive the boredom, frustration, and meaninglessness of his elders gripped his heart. The numbing anticipation of being nothing more than a cog in the machine, a faceless fragment of the technologically controlled mass age—this fear drove him from his parents' world in search of meaning, intensity, and community.

THE PSYCHEDELIC EXPERIENCE

It is characteristic of civilizations in process of deteriorating that forms of personal salvation multiple. As a society reaches the brink of dissolution, when it is no longer able to ignore the inconsistencies between its ideals and its performance, individuals seek personal satisfaction in a variety of ways. Some solace their fear of personal meaninglessness through commitment to the monoliths of commerce. As Thomas Merton observed, the dedication of General Electric officials makes Trappist devotion seem sandlot. Others desert the depersonalizing Establishment and search for private Nirvanas. Some abandon the need to choose, drifting from one immediate satisfaction to the next. Some turn to drugs; some to God; some to drugs and God.

At the heart of the Hippie experience was the sacramental use of drugs. Although the relatively harmless narcotic, marijuana, was the most widely used, it was the hallucinogenic drugs LSD (lysergic acid diethylamide) which produced the "psychedelic" (mind manifesting or consciousness expanding) experience. Exactly what happens during an LSD trip is hard to describe. According to reporters of the Hippie scene:

LSD produces an eight-to-twelve hour trip highlighted by profound changes in thought, mood and activity. Colors become heightened, sounds take on preternatural shades of meaning or unmeaning; the trip passenger feels he can see into his very brain cells, hear and feel his blood and lymph coursing through their channels.[3]

In general, the LSD experience consists of changes in perception, thought, mood, body, image and time. Colors intensify or change, shape and spatial relations appear distorted, objects seem to pulsate, and inanimate objects seem to assume emotional import. Sensitivity to sound increases, but the source of sound is elusive: conversations can be heard, for instance, but not comprehended. There may be auditory hallucination, or changes in taste. The subject may feel cold or sweaty. There are sensations of light-headedness, emptiness, shaking, vibrations, fogginess. Subjects lose awareness of their bodies with a resulting floating sensation. . . . Time seems to race, stop, slow down or even go backwards. Changes in thought include a free flow of bizarre ideas, and sometimes include notions of persecutions. Trivial events assume unnatural importance . . . inspiration or insight . . . is claimed. . . .[4]

Under the guidance of such Hippie gurus as Timothy Leary, the drug-induced state was interpreted as the attainment of a mystical vision of ultimate reality. LSD was used to still ordinary consciousness and enable the individual to step outside of himself. (We should recall that "standing outside of oneself" is precisely the etymology of the word "ecstasy.") Normal consciousness and the habitual subconscious associations of a lifetime are suspended. For example, the ringing of a bell no longer suggests a telephone which must be answered or a door which must be opened. This process of depersonalization or ego-loss was guided toward the attainment of a vision of the Real. The Tibetan *Book of the Dead*, which was recited to monks during their final hours to prepare them for the voyage of the soul, was reinterpreted by Leary and his associates as a manual for the dying ego, a guide to higher states of consciousness.

In the introduction to *Psychedelic Prayers*, Leary distinguishes three levels of psychedelic consciousness. First, there is the *neural* level reached by marijuana smokers, adepts in *hatha yoga*, and practitioners of Buddhist meditation. At the neural level the nerve energies are bombarded by raw energies. Acute perception of objects transcends the usual ego associations. Experience is enjoyed without the interference of concepts, symbols, and prejudices. Second, there is the *cellular* level. The sense organs are so overwhelmed by the acute perceptions of the neural level that their effects cancel one another. At this level the individual becomes aware of his own cellular processes. Finally, there is the *molecular* level which is attained through the use of large doses of LSD or other hallucinogenic agents. Leary identifies the molecular level with the oriental goal of the "white light" or "void." The molecular level is beyond sensory awareness, beyond cellular flow, and "in contact with the elemental energies that crackle and vibrate within the cellular structure."[5]

The Book of the Dead is divided into three sections or *Bardos*. As interpreted by Leary *et al.*, the First Bardo is concerned with the death of the ego and the experience of the great white light. The Second Bardo deals with drug-induced hallucinations. The LSD tripper is told that these may be terrifying or joyful. He is reminded that these

visions are products of his own mind, arbitrary combina-
tions of the categories and associations with which he or-
dinarily interprets his experience. He is told not to fear
them but to surrender and attend to the "Clear Light" behind them. The Third Bardo deals with the period of re-
entry, the recovery of consciousness by the ego.

Taken collectively, the three sections of the *Book of the
Dead* are used to structure the psychedelic experience as a
religious experience. But as the Hippies noted, "everyone
is on his own trip"—the LSD user was entitled to interpret
the experience as he saw fit. It is intention, associations,
community, and life consequences which make a given
experience religious. In other words, all the experiences of
a religious person are religious. Although many of the Hippies sought a drug-induced religious experience, they frequently rejected Leary's effort to force his trip on everyone.
Individual Hippies and Hippie communes which have
survived the death of Hippiedom have increasingly turned
away from drugs to the mind-expanding potentialities of
ordinary experience. Many Hippies have come to realize the
sacramental dimension, the numinous depths, the intense
satisfactions of their new, free life. Drugs have opened
their eyes but have not been necessary to sustain their vision.

THE HIPPIE "THEOLOGY"

The Hippies constituted a strange movement in which,
to quote observers, "scholars and thinkers of some eminence

find themselves marching more or less in step with such diverse elements as artists, clergymen, beatniks, and a host of youthful adherents whose motives range from a frivolous quest for kicks to a high-minded search for union with deity."[6] If this description is correct, the Hippie movement was no different from contemporary Christianity or a host of other reformation-inclined groups. From beginning to end, the motives of the various individuals who participate in any ideal-inspired movement are highly ambiguous. For this reason all such organizations are also ambiguous. Only a Pollyanna or a thorough cynic can deny that a mixture of high and shameful motivations bring men together in any mass movement.

My chief interest is those who pursued "a high-minded search for union with deity." What did they believe? What standards of behavior governed their lives? When I attempt to answer these questions, I encounter grave difficulties, for the "theology" of those who sought after the divine coun-selled silence regarding the nature or attributes of the object of their ecstatic vision. As is the case with most mystical religions, experience and not information were considered of utmost importance.

According to the Hippies, the psychedelic experience transcends every symbol, concept, or explanation. A reverent respect was demanded for the ineffability of both the aware-ness achieved and the presence disclosed through this ex-perience. The Hippies ransacked the congenial mystical traditions of the Orient—Upanishadic Hinduism, esoteric

Taoism, Zen Buddhism—for expressions of experiences which rupture the categories of the religious orthodoxies of the West. Because Judaism and Christianity have lost contact with their own mystical heritage, the clergymen who serve the Hippies' suburbanite parents have answered the seekers' requests for the bread of ecstatic experience with the stones of irrelevant religious doctrine.

In the Judaism and Christianity of their youth, the Hippies found only a societal religion which sanctified the status quo. The Hippies could not ignore the contradictions between what their parents believed and the way they lived, between the ethical standards enjoined by religion and the injustice which it condoned. But the pessimism, the cold and loveless cynicism of many young people was not their answer. Rather they attempted to fulfill the spirit of religion by a life of unbridled love. No matter how naive and inconsistent they may have been, the Hippies lived by a code of gentleness and brotherhood. They showed a deep concern for fellow Hippies, a reverence for nature, a compassion for all living things (which led many Hippies to become vegetarians), and a sense of identification with society's pariahs—the poor and the black.

The Hippies had many heroes and saints. Thoreau, Gandhi, Jesus, the Buddha, and St. Francis of Assisi—all of whom had dropped out of straight society in search of a transforming insight and then had opposed the Establishment for the sake of the insight which they had acquired— were universally revered. Contemporary personalities who had advocated the psychedelic experience were honored. The Hippies' favorite celebrities included author Aldous Huxley, who was in many ways psychedelia's John the Baptist; poet Allen Ginsberg, whose personal synthesis of drug-induced mysticism and Hindu ceremonialism exerted a powerful influence upon the Hippies; Timothy Leary, certainly the closest thing to Hippiedom's founder; and the Beatles, whose experimentation with drugs and Eastern meditation made them the cultural heroes *par excellence* of the Hippies.

For the Hippies, the discovery and actualization of one's true self was the way, the truth, and the life. The chief end of man is the progressive realization of one's unique self-hood—in Hippie argot, "doing your own thing." Once again the Hippies resorted to Eastern spirituality to express their basic intuition. They affirmed that the same divine presence which reveals itself as being, consciousness, and bliss in the psychedelic experience is the ground of all beings, the very core of each human personality. As the Hindu *Upanishads* proclaim, the Atman (true self) and Brahman (the divine Spirit) are identical. Each person is a never-to-be-repeated image of the hidden One, a unique and cherished reflection of the unitary Being which under-lies all things. Thus, the Hippies were *mystical panentheists*, attempting to realize in the celebration of each man's distinctness the ultimate harmony upon which all differences are based, the universal Spirit present in all things as the bearer of joy and meaning.

An aspect of the Hippies' mystical panentheism, which has spread throughout young America, is the dependence upon astrology. The popularity of astrology may be traced to many motives. According to a *Time* magazine feature article:

> Predictive astrology, like divination and occultism generally, tends to take hold in times of confusion, uncertainty and the breakdown of religious belief. Astrologers and assorted sorcerers were busy in Rome while the empire was declining and prevalent throughout Europe during the 17th century wave of plague. Today's young stargazers claim to be responding to a similar sense of disintegration and disenchantment.[7]

To traditional Western religion, with its emphasis on the responsibility of the individual for the transformation of his environment, interest in astrology must be condemned as a shirking of one's accountability for his own actions. There is no doubt that many young people (and not-so-young people) have found in the stars what they formerly found in Freudianism—an inscrutable determinism which can be blamed for every misfortune, whether self-inflicted or circumstantial.

But we must remember that a sense of helplessness, a consciousness that the fate of the individual is not under his control, is not only epidemic but irrefutable. Is it possible to entertain the notion of freedom and responsibility in the face of the utter irrationality of modern life? It is not easy for a young adult who has been the victim of whim and caprice throughout his academic years, who trusts more in "the breaks" than in the equity of the forces that govern his life, to believe the Renaissance myth that each of us stands at the center of his own universe and determines his own fate. Perhaps our fate is not in ourselves but in our stars, after all.

And yet we do serious injustice to the Hippie dependence upon astrology if we see it only as an abdication of responsibility. For the Hippies, astrology was much more than arcane fortune-telling. It was the expression of a mystical participation in the unity of all things. Marshall McLuhan views the current interest of youth in astrology, clairvoyance, and the occult as the first stage in the "demise of spoken language and its replacement by a global consciousness."[8] According to McLuhan, "Psychic communal integration, made possible at last by the electronic media, could create the universality of consciousness foreseen by Dante when he predicted that men would continue as no more than broken fragments until they were unified into an inclusive consciousness."[9] But apart from McLuhan's vision of the future, we can sympathize with the unitary mysticism of the Hippies. If reality is a seamless Whole, an essential Harmony in which every part affects and is affected by every other part, then man cannot be unaffected by the stars and planets. To the Hippie, astrology was not so much a science as a reaffirmation of the fundamental Oneness of reality.

HIPPIE COMMUNITY

If each man is a unique manifestation of a unitary ground, then each should seek to contribute his distinctness to the creation of community in order to manifest that essential unity. I strongly suspect that the successes and failures of Hippie communalism, their efforts at the attainment of actual community, will form their greatest legacy to the future. The history of Hippie communalism will be probed by social scientists long after the artifacts of Hippie culture have faded from view.

The Hippie concern for community initially grew from a regard for "where, when, and with whom you trip." The importance of preparation received an emphasis similar to the matter of purification in the rites of primitive religions. Inadequate preparation for the psychedelic experience was considered foolhardy from the beginning of the psychedelic movement. As Richard Alpert, Leary's earliest associate stated: "I take LSD only when I feel ready and in a setting I feel is supportive."[10] Leary frequently chided those who professed disappointment with the results of an LSD trip: "Did you expect to find God at the end of a needle?"[11]

The basis of Hippie community was the psychedelic religious experience, an extrovertive mysticism which heightened sensory awareness, producing a delight for sight, sound, odor, taste, and touch which far outlasted the LSD trip. The Hippie rediscovered the body and its senses. His way of life celebrated a virtual resurrection of the body, an acceptance of sensual beauty and physical pleasure which contrasted sharply with the inherent antiaesthetic and antisexual tendencies of western religion. But Hippie expressions of the free life of the turned-on senses were never unrestrained. The Hippie insistence that each man be allowed to "do his own thing" was counterbalanced with the disdain for uncontrolled and irresponsible actions which would harm other members of the community. Unfortunately such concern did not extend to the individual. The drug-induced loss of ego often lengthened into a tragic, permanent escape from reality. The Hippie ethic required that all members be warned of the dangers attendant upon the use of a given drug, but it did not extend to community interdiction of any one's trip.

The spirit of the Hippies, symbolized in the familiar and abused world "love," was explained by Leary in an interview for one of the "underground" newspapers: "We are not a religion in the sense of the Methodist Church seeking new adherents. We're a religion in the basic primeval sense of a tribe living together and centered around shared spiritual goals. So you can't join our religion any more than you can join a tribe. . . ."[12]

The various forms of social life among the Hippies were reminiscent of America's great utopian experiments and voluntary communities. Hippie communes ranged from Drop City near Trinidad, Colorado, with its score of writers, painters, and general scroungers, to the Eleventh Street Diggers' Commune on New York's Lower East Side, which provided shelter and guidance for hundreds of runaways and dropouts. Soup kitchens, clinics, the Neo-American Church, impromptu concerts, Hippie "non-families" of cottage artists, the Hip Job Coop, were only a few manifestations of an acute sense of community. At their zenith, the Hippies formed an international community of communes—each different from its counterparts; yet each an embodiment of identical Hippie values.

Inner Space, the first monthly "magazine of the Psychedelic community," spawned more than fifty underground newspapers which served Hippiedom as an outlet for creative (often obscene) energies, while fulfilling the usual functions of the press—news coverage, advice to the lovelorn (and drug-worn), letters to the editors, etc. The Hippie free press movement was but another example of a striving after solidarity. The Hippie was not content to reject American conventionality. In its place he offered what he considered a viable alternative, an all-embracing style of life. The Hippie desired a community that permitted him to "do his own thing" within a supportive brotherhood which shared his ideals, his aspirations, and, above all, his religious experience.

THE FUTURE?

What is the future of the psychedelic movement? The Hippie has been replaced by the pseudo-Hippie, the plastic Hippie, the weekend Hippie, and adolescents who buy their Hippie costumes at Korvette's. Hippiedom died just as Christendom did when everyone converted. An entire generation of young people adopted the Hippie garb but not the Hippie life style. Long hair, surplus store clothing, beads, and sandals no more make a person a Hippie than a red hat makes a man a cardinal. The religious Hippies have gone into retreat. Some are hiding in foreign lands. Others have taken up residence on Hippie farms in remote parts of America. Many are invisible in our midst, a beard-less and sandalless Fifth Column within straight society.

The Hippie has left the scene and the "new man" is taking his place. The hedonistic cults are at the center of the stage, the dance gets wilder, the music louder, the lights more intense, all restraint goes. The new man has drugs, social ideas, and a gun. His prototypes are the anarchistic "crazies" of the New Left and the drug-crazed hooligans on motorcycles. The new man is not content to follow the benign path of the Hippie. He is determined to outrage and destroy the society which produced him. The Hippie response to society was catatonic. He dropped out to regain the lost innocence of childhood. The new man—

the guerillas of the New Left and the Hell's Angels—is a psychotic. Violence is his sacrament. He chooses to allow the Establishment no recourse but repression. For repression will eventually destroy all that is precious in the American experience. The new man lures America toward Armageddon. He maximizes the tensions between groups, ages, and races. He propels us toward irreconcilable polarization. His program is to despise us and outrage us into irrational retaliation. Will we swallow the bait? Will we abandon the path of moderation, reason, and persuasion? In the moment we yield to the provocations of the new man, we will write "finis" to the American dream.

The Hippie phenomenom was a warning. It revealed the dissatisfaction of our youth with our materialism, our hypocrisies, our toleration of mediocrity and injustice. In some measure the Hippies expanded our minds, reawakened our senses and sensuality, reminded us of our own hunger for the experience of a living God. At least they have forbidden us to cry peace where there is no peace. But because we regarded them as only an amusing and bizarre fad, we never took the time to deal with the questions they raised. We belittled them as if they were nothing more than spoiled children. We presented them on television and in the movies as filthy, mindless criminals or idealistic crackpots. We hated them because they were young, because they were getting away with a libertarianism which we had neither the opportunity nor the guts to attempt, and because we produced them. Look at what a failure to understand one's offspring has done to the humanitarian spirit of Al Capp. His constant attack upon the young is both sick and typical.

The Hippies were neither a fraternity of saints nor an assemblage of self-pitying brats—and yet they were both. Hippiedom is dead. But their questions remain.

NOTES

[1] Lewis S. Feuer, *The Conflict of Generations: The Character and Significance of Student Movements* (New York: Basic Books, 1969).

[2] Review of Feuer, *op. cit., The New York Times Book Review* (March 30, 1969), p. 32.

[3] Joe David Brown, ed., "The Flower Children." Reprinted from *The Hippies* by the Editors of *Time* magazine, Time–Life Books, © 1967, Time, Inc., p. 11.

[4] Adrienne Pauly, *ibid.*, p. 192.

[5] T. Leary, *Psychedelic Prayers* (Kerhonkson, N.Y.; Poets Press, 1966).

[6] R. E. L. Master and Jean Houston, *The Varieties of Psychedelic Experience* (New York: Dell Publishing., 1967), p. 57.

[7] *Time* (March 21, 1969), p. 48.

[8] *Playboy* (March 1969), p. 72.

[9] *Ibid.*

[10] Richard Alpert, Sidney Cohen, and Lawrence Schiller, *LSD* (New York: New American Library, 1966), p. 30.

[11] Leary, "An Evening with God," public address at Village Theatre, N.Y., May 13, 1967.

[12] *Yarrowstalks*, No. 2, Philadelphia (August 1967).

4

<<<<<<<<<<<<<<<<<<<<<<<<<<<<<<<<<<<<<<<<<<<<<<<<<<

The Buddha's Path of Selfless Ecstasy

"THE BUDDHIST POINT of view will appeal only to those people who are completely disillusioned with the world as it is, and with themselves, who are extremely sensitive to pain, suffering and any kind of turmoil, who have an extreme desire for happiness, and a considerable capacity for renunciation."[1] If this authority is correct, then many of my best friends are Buddhists! For disillusionment with the world and one's own life, consciousness that life is not what it should be, and a fervent desire for contentment characterizes most sensitive individuals. The final hallmark, "a considerable capacity for renunciation," may be somewhat rarer—but it is hardly uncommon. Haven't we all become Jobs during the past thirty years? Life has become a pretty grim business. Tens of millions of innocent men, women, and children have been systematically exterminated like so many insects. Several times that number are doomed to death by slow starvation. Hundreds of thousand of young lives have been consumed in senseless wars which have left a harvest of inhumanity, barbarism, cruelty, and injustice.

The United States of America, the strongest and wealthiest nation in the history of mankind, is a land of poisoned air and polluted water, of racial strife and rampant crime, of personal instability and interpersonal alienation, of ulcers and divorce. To be an American is to be beset by skyrocketing expectations, hopeless dreams, and insatiable appetites. For the foundation of "the American way of life" is the advertiser's hollow promises of eternal youth, instant success, and sexual irresistibility—all for the price of a pack of cigarettes, a tube of toothpaste, an aerosol can of deodorant, or a bottle of mouthwash.

We are witnessing the inevitable Buddhizing of the West, the reenactment of the ordeal of Siddhartha Gautama, the founder of Buddhism, by thousands upon thousands of disillusioned moderns. Amidst the prosperity, opportunities, and pleasures of life in the secular city, a sizable minority drawn from every class, race, and age group importunes: "Stop the world. I want to get off."

Born in about 560 B.C., Siddhartha was the son of the ruler of a petty kingdom which embraced portions of what is today northeastern India and Nepal. Guided by a prophecy that the young prince would either become a world conqueror or a world savior, Siddhartha's father scrupulously shielded him from the facts of human suffering. But despite his father's precautions, Siddhartha encountered "the Four Passing Sights" which his father's seers had predicted. On successive chariot rides through the royal park, Siddhartha saw a decrepit old man, a man suffering from a fatal disease, a dead body, and an ascetic monk. From "The Four Passing Sights" he learned that all men are subject to age, sickness, sorrow, and death. The final sign—the yellow-robed, shaven-headed, mendicant recluse —so moved him that he resolved to forsake his father's court, his princely prerogatives, his wife and infant son for "the homeless state." Siddhartha was twenty-nine when he went forth to seek deliverance from the sorrows of human existence. For six years he lived by the strictest ascetic disciplines, subjecting both body and mind to the cruelest self-mortifications. But he found nothing to assuage his desperate craving for contentment.

Only when he surrendered the severities of the ascetic quest, when he gave up the effort to overcome the ignorance and desire which bind each man to the path of endless travail—in this moment he became the *Buddha*, the Enlightened One, the Man Who Woke Up. It is not possible for us to gain access to the transforming experience. What happened to Siddhartha Gautama as he sat in contemplation at the root of a tree was something unique, private, and unrepeatable. And yet it is the goal for which all men strive. Siddhartha had become a *Jina*, one who has overcome all passion, delusion, and ignorance. Exactly what happened, no one will ever know. For such personal bliss is incommunicable.

What then was so significant about this moment under the Botree? Why have men turned by the tens of millions to this mysterious figure? The most intense and significant experience of a man's life may be inexpressible but it is never without consequences. How poor is language for the expression of that which a man holds most dear, that which has made him the person he is. But if there is any real value to his transformation, it will be contagious. So it was with the Buddha.

Although he was content with his victory, the Enlightened One was moved by compassion for his fellows. According to an ancient legend, Mara (the tempter) invited him to enter the eternal bliss which he had attained. But the Buddha's pity for those who yet suffered led him to reply: "I will first establish in perfect wisdom worlds as numerous as the sand, and then will I enter Nirvana (the state of final bliss)."

From the tree of enlightenment, the Buddha traveled to Benares where he began his public ministry. In his first sermon, delivered to five ascetic monks in the deer park near Benares, he declared the Four Noble Truths which are the foundation of Buddhism. In the following paragraphs I have presented these teachings together with some explanatory comments. (The translation of the Buddha's sermon combines several standard translations of this portion of the Mahavagga.)

THE FIRST AND SECOND
NOBLE TRUTHS

(1) This is the Noble Truth of Suffering: Birth is suffering; old age is suffering; illness is suffering; death is suffering. Sorrow, lamentation, dejection, and despair are suffering. Contact with unpleasant things is suffering; not getting what we desire is suffering.

(2) This is the Noble Truth of the Cause of Suffering: Suffering originates in craving . . . accompanied by pleasure and lust, finding its delight here and there. This thirst is threefold: thirst for pleasure, thirst for existence, thirst for prosperity.

When the Western reader first confronts the message of the Buddha, he automatically exclaims: "What pessimism! To think that millions of human beings have sought refuge in a religion based on the belief that the sum and substance of human experience is pain, sorrow, and grief." We are willing to admit that suffering is present in every life, that it is an element in virtually every human endeavor—individual or corporate. But something deep inside resists the suggestion that suffering is ultimate.

Western philosophers and theologians have never tired of the effort to explain and justify human suffering. They have argued that pain is remedial, or character-strengthening, or redemptive, or the price of admission to a better world hereafter. And even though their arguments fail to convince those of us who are neither philosophers nor theologians, we manage to believe that life makes sense despite the heartaches and the thousand natural shocks that flesh is heir to. We tell ourselves that death, pain, sorrow, and grief are only temporary; that they are only the dark hues which the divine artist uses to give contrast to the brighter portions of his canvas; that they are punishment for our own wilful abuse of our freedom as created beings; that they produce maturity and compassion. But must we not rebel at the justice of the divine bookkeeper? Can we overlook the obvious facts that the unrighteous prosper while the good are deprived, hounded, and murdered before our very eyes? And so we tell ourselves that there is a final judgment, a postmortem review, an ultimate justification of the senselessness of life.

The remarkable thing is that most of us believe that pain, sorrow, and evil make sense. In a time of widespread dissatisfaction with all religion, we persistently cling to the conviction that the world is basically sane, rational, and good. For none of us want to live in a world governed by caprice, irrationality, and absurdity. We recoil from the inexplicable, the senseless, and the unfathomable. We do so not because we believe in a just and loving God who controls the affairs and destiny of mankind, but because we are terrified at the prospect that the world of our every-day experience may turn to be what we know ourselves to be: incomprehensible, senseless, and cruel. And who could live with such a realization? Who would want to pursue a socially productive career, raise children, plan for the future, attempt to contribute to the well-being of his fellows, if he really knew in his heart of hearts that all is futile, that nothing makes sense?

Can it be that the Buddha is right? That our sublime optimism is based on a delusion? That we believe what we have to believe in order to find the courage to face another day? Perhaps the First Noble Truth is the expression of a profound realism rather than of a despairing pessimism. For if a man is to improve himself and the conditions in which he lives, he must first see them as they really are. He must take off the blinders of unwarranted expectations. He must accept the unpalatable facts without the sugar-coating of childhood truisms. He must admit that his most frequent prayer during his adult life has been "God have mercy upon us"—the petition which he finds the most appropriate to the circumstances of modern life and the most relevant to his own actions.

To be a human being is to suffer—this is the first word from "the One Who Woke Up." But a man or woman does not have to be a Buddhist to realize that the message of the Buddha is irrefutable. Even a young man who is still delighted with life, eager for challenges and adventures, grateful to be loved, full of dreams and hopes, cannot controvert the First Noble Truth. For he was born against his will, screaming in terror. Day by day, he is oppressed by the consciousness of his mortality, forced to live with death as an ever-present possibility. He is compelled to witness the gradual decay of his own body and mind, the remorseless withering away of his capacity for joy, the shrinkage of compassion, the inadequacies of his understanding. Every day brings greater and greater burdens of responsibility, possibilities for mistakes, a deeper sense of frustration, an awareness of powerlessness, a gnawing conviction of personal guilt.

Nor is life different for the mature and respected. The sensitive and talented are wasted in petty bureaucracies, confounded by the vagaries of fate, and threatened by their own innate weaknesses. The essential anxiety and loneliness of modern man sends him into a frenzy of activity which from the very beginning is doomed to futility. The realization that whether we are saints or bastards, we are all bound to lose has prompted tens of thousands to drop out. Our work-and-success obsessed culture must judge the non-achiever harshly, for he makes us aware of the obvious: *Most of us would join him if we could.*

But why is human experience painful from beginning to end? If the Buddha had been an American, he might have formulated the Second Noble Truth as follows: The basic cost of living is 110 percent of income. Above ten thousand dollars per annum, the cost of essentials is 120 percent. And so forth. Thus, the greater one's income, the more impoverished one becomes. A millionaire deprived of a yacht suffers as intensely as a poor woman who cannot afford a second dress.

According to the Second Noble Truth, the cause of suffering is desire, for it is impossible to satisfy fully even the most elemental craving. The moment a man obtains what he wants, he fears that he will lose it. Or he discovers that it is inadequate. Or he feels guilty for depriving another of happiness for the sake of his pleasure. As Edward Conze observes: "Roast duck is pleasant as long as one ignores the feelings of the duck."

We Americans are well aware that the problem is not to get what we want but to want what we get. In our remarkably mobile society, an individual can have practically anything he wants. Anyone can become President, own two houses, vacation in Acapulco, write a bestselling novel, drive a sports car. But to have something and to be content with it are two different things. For to possess is to be possessed. *Blessed is he who owns everything, for he shall be servant of all!* Nothing is properly made. The quest for adequate repair is hopeless. No appliance, item of apparel, professional service, domicile, personal relationship, vocational opportunity, or recreational activity is worth the frustrations, annoyances, and inconveniences of having it.

THE THIRD AND FOURTH
NOBLE TRUTHS

(3) *This is the Noble Truth of the Cessation of suffering:* *Suffering ceases with the complete cessation of desire—a*

cessation which consists in the absence of every passion—
with the abandoning of this desire, with the doing away
with it, with the deliverance from it, with the destruction
of desire.

(4) This is the Noble Truth of the Path which leads to the
cessation of suffering: the holy eightfold Path—right views,
right intention, right speech, right action, right livelihood,
right effort, right mindfulness, right meditation.

The attainment of personal enlightenment requires not
only that one know the truth but that one do something
about it. It is not sufficient to know the path to liberation.
It is necessary to follow it. The starting point is an awareness of the world and of one's own self as they really are.
The Buddhist attitude on these two subjects may be sum-
marized by two related concepts: anicca (impermanence)
and anatta (selflessness). According to the Buddha, the
reason for suffering is man's ignorance of the real condition
of his existence. Nothing could be surer to us than the
existence of the world of our everyday experience. We are
aware of ourselves and a world to which we belong. I know
myself as the subject of my own acts, thoughts, dreams,
feelings, etc. Through the empirical senses of sight, hearing,
touch, smell, and taste I come to know the various objects
which make up my environment: other selves, trees, sky,
automobiles, houses, clothing, food, and so forth. Nothing
could be more indubitable. My every thought, utterance,
and deed presuppose these primal verities: my own exist-

ence and the trustworthy world of my experience. Alas, says the Buddha, both are illusory.

As a Christian hymn proclaims, "Time like an ever-rolling stream bears all her sons away." Our thoughts and memories are just so many still photographs of a dynamic, ever-changing flux. We have grown so accustomed to these static images that we confuse them with reality, just as the eye is fooled into perceiving motion when a rapid succession of pictures is projected on a screen. But when we stop and consider the matter carefully, we realize that nothing is constant, changeless, or trustworthy. From moment to moment, all of reality undergoes ceaseless transformation. We tend to overlook the impermanence of everything around us, just as we ignore our own day-by-day transfiguration from youth to old age. Only when the unanticipated occurs—when a man is unable to lift a burden that he has carried a thousand times, when a person who has been a fixture in our lives is suddenly removed by death, when our children reject the commonplaces upon which we have depended—only then do we suddenly face up to the impermanence of all things.

We all know that we are not today the persons that we were ten years ago. We have matured or soured; found new direction or become hopelessly disillusioned; been converted or become indifferent; found out what life is all about or come to know better than to ask. Perhaps each is the case in one way or another. But no matter how much we have changed, each of us still believes that he or she is the same person. Despite all the changes that have taken place, it is *I* who have changed—the selfsame, identical *I*. And each of us insists that the same is true for all other selves. No matter how greatly a man is altered from day to day, he is *essentially* the same—or so we believe. After all, the debts which I incurred yesterday are my obligations today. Unless I desire to renounce my humanity by being declared insane, I must accept the consequences of my words and deeds even though I will be a different man in a few hours. Of course, it is to my benefit to accept the casual assumptions of permanence. How could I manage if the salary which I earned this month were withheld on the grounds that I was no longer the man who earned it? Or if my doctorate were cancelled due to changes in my basic attitudes toward the philosophy of religion subsequent to the fulfillment of the degree requirements? Such conditions would be intolerable. Yes, I have changed in the past ten years but, nevertheless, it is *I* who have changed.

According to Buddhist teachings, the belief that my experiences, thoughts, feelings, and memories are really *my* experiences, thoughts, feelings, and memories is the result of a firmly established habit. Through the constant use of such words as "I," "my," "me," and "mine," the illusion arises that there is an actual entity corresponding to these words. The reification of such language creates the impression that there are separate selves. The habitual usage of personal nouns and pronouns is so deeply entrenched that the belief in separate selves is a *necessary* error. If the consequences of this mistake were merely academic, they would be of no concern. But, according to the Buddhist, belief in a substantial self is the root of all ignorance, pain, and suffering. Conversely, the reversal of this standpoint is the source of man's redemption.

The *Dhammapada* (The Path of Righteousness), Buddhism's most revered sacred writing, declares: "All that we are is the result of what we have thought: it is founded on our thoughts, it is made up of our thoughts. If a man speaks or acts with an evil thought, pain follows him, as the wheel follows the foot of the ox that draws the carriage. . . . If a man speaks or acts with a pure thought, happiness follows him, like a shadow that never leaves him" (trans. Friedrich Max Müller). If a man believes that he is his consciousness and experience, then he will both suffer and cause suffering. For the day by day, moment by moment changes which he perceives in his consciousness of himself will bring him pain. His senses will tell him that he is ageing, that his body is decaying, that he is approaching the termination of his existence, that whatever goods or pleasures he possesses are fleeting things. Thus, despair, anxiety, and sorrow are the lot of the one who constantly entertains the error of his separate existence.

But the pain does not end here. For belief in a self gives birth to self-centeredness, to self-assertion, to the numberless efforts to preserve and enhance one particular self at the cost of all other selves. As each man's egocentricity has separated him from and set him against all other men, the evils which haunt our social existence have arisen. As the wheel follows the foot of the ox, so have poverty, theft, violence, slander, and immorality followed the fundamental error of self-devotion. Selfishness—in forms which range from insensitivity to the needs of one's neighbor to the deliberate annihilation of human life and potential by the totally egotistic individual—destroys perpetrator and victim alike.

Since the consequences of belief in separate selves are more serious than the belief, it is not sufficient to correct the idea. The effects must also be overcome. A pragmatic program of radical selflessness is required. Buddhism advocates both *extrovertive* and *introvertive* techniques for the achievement of selflessness. According to the former, the individual is encouraged to conquer the illusion of separate selfhood by a life of compassionate service for all. Santideva, a Buddhist sage who live about A.D. 600, instructed men as follows:

By pondering in such wise . . . a man stills vain imaginations and strengthens his thought of Enlightenment. First he will diligently foster the thought that his fellow-creatures are the same as himself. "All have the same sorrows, the same joys as I, and I must guard them like myself. The body, manifold of parts in its division of members, must be preserved as a whole; and so likewise this manifold universe has its sorrow and its joy in common. . . . I must destroy the pain of another as though

it were my own. . . . I must show kindness to others, for
they are creatures as I myself . . ."2

When I realize that the boundaries between separate selves
are only illusions, I come to know that the elimination of
my suffering can be accomplished only by the removal of all
suffering.

A poignant expression of the path of selfless compassion
is found in the *Bodhisattva* ideal. A Bodhisattva, one who is
about to become a Buddha, postpones his entrance into
nirvana so that he may lead others to perfection. Following
the example of Gautama, a Bodhisattva vows to take upon
himself the whole burden of human suffering in order that
others may be saved. Although he has accomplished the
practices which lead to full enlightenment, the Bodhisattva
surrenders his own life and pleasures that he may bring all to
final bliss. By his compassionate oneness with others, the
Bodhisattva loses any thought of his separate existence.
But, paradoxically, the Bodhisattva's very renunciation of
nirvana for the sake of others demonstrates that he has
attained beatitude. The *Lankavatara Sutra* affirms:

> . . . when the Bodhisattvas face and perceive the happiness
> of the samadhi of perfect tranquillization [i.e., the ecstasy
> of selfless meditation discussed below], they are moved
> with the feeling of love and sympathy owing to their
> original vows . . . made for all beings, saying, 'So long as
> they do not attain Nirvana I will not attain it myself.'

Thus they keep themselves away from Nirvana. But the fact
is that they are already in Nirvana because in them there
is no rising of discrimination [i.e., the discernment of
separate selves].[3]

By identifying with the sorrows and heartaches of all beings,
the Bodhisattva transcends the error of self-affirmation in
actuality rather than merely in theory.

Another illustration of the extrovertive path is the culti-
vation of a sense of unity with nature which is so characteristic of Chinese and Japanese Buddhism. According to the
Meditation School of Buddhism (*Ch'an* or *Zen* Buddhism
in China and Japan, respectively), enlightenment comes
when a man transcends the conceptual schemes which
separate him from reality. Man must find his place in the
natural order, his essential identity with all things. Western
art is anthropocentric. Man stands at the center as the
measure of all things. Hindu art is theocentric, portraying
the gods in all their terrible awesomeness. But the art of
Buddhism depicts man, the natural sphere and ultimate
reality with each in proper perspective. Ninian Smart
observes:

Tender and mysterious landscapes depict the peaks of
upward-soaring, indented mountains, with here and there
a pine or a cedar. Far below there is a man fishing. In
between there is the great misty blank of the valley. If we
look objectively at the scroll, we perceive that a vast part

of it is simply blank. The painter achieves much of his effect by not painting. . . .⁴

Man is neither the center of the universe (as Western art presupposes) nor is he totally insignificant (as Hindu art suggests). He is a part of a harmonious One. But even this balanced universe is not the final truth. For at the center of all things is a void. Not by effort nor prayer nor faith but only by renunciation of every self-centered act can the ultimate be reached.

The extrovertive way finds emphasis in *Mahayana* ("Great Vehicle"), the predominant school of Buddhism which has flourished at various times in China, Japan, Korea, and Tibet. *Theravada* ("The Tradition of the Elders"), the Buddhism of Ceylon, Burma, East Pakistan, and Thailand, stresses a more introvertive path to selfless-ness. And yet the two approaches are completely compatible. Both schools are united in their effort to attain personal enlightenment by following the way of the Buddha. But Mahayanist and Theravadin emulation of the *Tathagata* ("the One Who has Arrived [at the Truth]," "the One Who has Broken Through") focuses upon two complementary but divergent traits of the Buddha-character. As conceived by all Buddhists, the Buddha combines in his being both Wisdom and Compassion. Although these characteristics may be distinguished, they are essentially inseparable and mutually inclusive. To know the real is to become real. The compassion of the Buddha is both the consequence and proof of his Widsom.

Wisdom (*panna*), as the term is used in Buddhism, does not refer to intellectual understanding but rather to the actual destruction of ignorance and its effects. It is never enough to grasp the truth. To be wise is to be grasped by the truth. Wisdom is not information but escape from a lesser to a fuller state of existence. Although Wisdom infinitely transcends right opinions and rules of behavior, it includes both. Wrong convictions, and the actions which follow from them, are obstacles to enlightenment. Unless a man restrains from violence, theft, immorality, and intoxication, he will remain fettered to the world of pain and sorrow. Therefore, the Buddhist must refrain from certain occupations (e.g., public executioner, prostitute, wine merchant). He must zealously guard against attitudes such as lust, ill will, sloth, anxiety, and doubt which reveal bondage to the self-centered state. His every thought, word, and deed must be directed by the awareness of the impermanence and insufficiency of all things.

But the precepts and principles of the path of Wisdom are only a preparation for its goal: the ecstasy of selfless meditation. It is to this consummation that the other seven steps of the Eightfold Path lead. *Right views, right intention, right speech, right action, right livelihood, right effort, and right mindfulness* prepare the individual for the beatitude of ego-transcending concentration. All schools of Buddhism teach that few have the capacity for the experience of final bliss. And yet, Buddhists believe that *nirvana* awaits all men, that the Buddha-nature is hidden within each of us. The contradiction between the beliefs that (a) few are capable of enlightenment; and (b) enlightenment is the destiny of every man is resolved by the doctrine of rebirth. Countless lifetimes are required for the extinction of all desire and the cessation of the sufferings instigated by pain. Those few who have attained *nirvana*, the selfless state in which all desire has ceased, demonstrate that sorrow will be overcome and bliss attained by everyone.

All religions enjoin men to seek salvation through prayer, works, or faith. But Buddhism sees these as lesser means, tools which even the Buddha employs in his skill and tact to wean men away from the wretchedness of finite things. Buddhism has always found a place for those who turned to the Buddha as to a saving deity, who called on his name, trusted in him for refuge. At the same time, Buddhism has never forgotten that the experience of the Buddha was of utmost importance. Veneration, ceremony, and devotion are acceptable for the purpose of calling attention to the immanent Buddhahood of every human being. In the end, each of us must duplicate for himself the enlightenment of Siddhartha Gautama. Hence, Buddhism presents a discipline of rigorous self-control through which "the body is subdued, the instincts are weakened, the mind is calmed, logical thinking is baffled and exhausted by absurdities, and sensory facts are thought little of, the eye of faith and the eye of wisdom replacing the eyes of the body."[5]

In discussing the path to selfless ecstasy, it is absolutely necessary to distinguish between the techniques of right meditation and *nirvana*, the goal of such meditation. *Nirvana* is no more produced by the strenuous self-disciplines of right meditation than a mountain is produced by walking the road which leads to it. A traveller may find his way to a particular place, even though he ignores the directions of those who have been there before him. But if he does so, there is always the possibility that he will never attain his goal. According to the *Dhammapada*, the Eightfold Path is "the best of ways." If followed exactly, it will always lead to freedom and bliss. But the same document states that even the Buddha is only a guide. Each of us must make the journey for himself.

The ultimate destiny of each life is *nirvana*, which the Buddhist scriptures describe as the extinction of all desires (and, thus, of all suffering), the overcoming of error and hatred, the uprooting of attachment, the attainment of Wisdom and calm. In the words of a Buddhist monk, Walpola Rahula:

He who has realized . . . Nirvana is the happiest being in the world. He is free from all "complexes" and obsessions, the worries and troubles that torment others. His mental health is perfect. He does not repent the past, nor does he brood over the future. He lives fully in the present. Therefore he appreciates and enjoys things in the purest sense. . . . He is joyful, exultant, enjoying the pure life, his faculties pleased, free from anxiety, serene and peaceful. As he is free from selfish desire, hatred, ignorance, conceit, pride, and all such "defilements," he is pure and gentle, full of universal love, compassion, kindness, sympathy, understanding and tolerance.[6]

In sum, the man who has attained nirvana has fulfilled the requirements for perfect humanity—not just the Buddhist requirements but those of every religion and humanistic philosophy. Who could quibble with such an ideal of human destiny? But the remarkable thing about Buddhism is that it believes that nirvana may be achieved before death. Further, and even more remarkable, it teaches a practical path of self-culture by which a man may remove the obstacles to his final goal and at the same time enjoy concrete benefits even if he never attains that goal during his lifetime.

In order to comprehend the personal liberation achieved by right concentration, I invite the reader to engage in an experiment based on two widely practiced techniques of Buddhist meditation: breath consciousness and presentness.

(a) Breath consciousness. Sit erect in a comfortable chair or cross-legged on the floor. Close your eyes or allow them to stare into the distance, whichever you find most comfortable. Now breathe as you normally do; but pay close attention to your breathing. Concentrate fully as you inhale and exhale. Forget about your surroundings, the cares of the day, the sounds from the street, and all other impressions. Concentrate only on each breath. Continue for five or ten minutes. Repeat the exercise twice daily for several days.

At first, the mind wanders. The sounds, sights, odors, and feel of your surroundings impinge upon your attention. Your attention wanders away from breath consciousness to entertain memories, resolve personal problems, wonder about all that annoys and perplexes you. But gradually the world of the senses disappears. Thoughts, memories, and feelings give way to rapt contemplation upon each inhalation and exhalation. You lose yourself completely in the awareness of your breathing. In those rare moments when the world of the everyday ceases to exist, you experience a joy and tranquility as complete as you have ever known. All because you have focussed your total attention upon a simple, mundane act.

By living fully in the present—neither in the past with its regrets nor the future with it uncertainties—one can attain a foretaste of final bliss in every experience. By attending to one's actions, fully enjoying them here and now, it is possible to free the mind of worry, the body of tension, and the spirit of impediments to its upward quest. Breath consciousness is a simple application of right meditation. After one has learned to concentrate fully upon this activity, he may turn to any other. He may develop an all-embracing sense of presentness.

(b) *Presentness.* Our ordinary awareness of the world imprisons us in the solitude of inner experience. We deal with reality only indirectly, through abstractions, concepts, memories, and previously observed relationships. The vitality of the real is captured in static generalizations, like an insect trapped in amber. But the development of a sense of presentness allows objects, persons, and relationships to glow with the force of the here and now. By becoming fully mindful of each experience, self-consciousness fades away. When I play my guitar, fully absorbed in playing, I experience a joyous freedom. But when my attention shifts to my audience, I become aware of myself— the esteem with which I am held, the degree to which I am appreciated—and my contentment turns into sheer terror. To give one's self fully to the task at hand, to experience the joy of the moment, is to lose one's self completely. And the joyous loss of the self is precisely the consummation which mankind devoutly seeks.

A craving for presentness is apparent throughout our culture. We witness it in the phenomenal growth of "encounter groups." By the application of an exotic balm concocted of one part psychodrama, one part group dynamics, one part bull session, and one part pure exhibitionism, tens of thousands of Americans are seeking a recovery of awareness, a rebirth of the senses. Although the burgeoning and variegated "encounter movement" is distinctively Western in its understanding of the causes and cure of the human predicament, it freely adopts techniques from Eastern religions. But the faddistic use of Buddhist and Hindu jargon should not blind us to the essentially non-oriental character of the movement.

Western man increasingly finds himself estranged from his body, his environment, and his neighbor. Neither present attainments nor future prospects can banish the gnawing sense of loneliness, the recurrent feeling of disjointedness. Man's control of his environment—his successful exploitation of his own resources and those of his fellows, his ability to manipulate personality through the techniques of market analysis, political propaganda, and psychological conditioning—has imprisoned him in the dreadful solitude of his role as omnipotent manager.

The various encounter groups are a response to this situation. They promise instant interpersonal relations, immediate self-knowledge, direct confrontation with reality. According to a *Newsweek* special report, one prominent psychologist observes approvingly that the encounter groups "are helping break through the alienation and dehumanization of our culture." But another authority notes: "Encounter groups are like a new religious cult. They have uniforms and ceremonies and cult leaders. It's a religion in the worst sense; you do it on Sunday and then forget it for the rest of the week."[7]

The drug culture of the young is a close parallel. Although such motivating factors as sheer hedonism, adolescent curiosity, and the magnetic attraction of any forbidden fruit cannot be discounted, the drug scene is fundamentally concerned with "the expansion of human consciousness"—a catch phrase which cloaks a multitude of sins and attracts countless novices to the cruelest of fates.

The expectation that chemical agents can restore or enhance awareness reiterates the problem of our times. For faith in drugs both affirms and denies the value of our technologically based urban existence. After all, the most potent mind-manifesting substances are synthesized. Whether or not drugs can reawaken our senses, heal our schizoid life style, harmonize our productive minds with our fallow bodies, or renew our sensitivities to the common sorrows of humanity, it is significant that hundreds of thousands expect them to.

The nirvana which we seek is vastly different than the goal of the Eightfold Path. The self-awareness, trained sensitivity, and interpersonal relatedness that we so actively cultivate sound suspiciously like the manipulative, means-end orientation which depersonalized us in the first place. Drugs and groups are part of our egocentric quest for a magic power over ourselves, our world, our fellows. But such solutions only widen the gaps between mind and body, man and man, mankind and nature.

Nirvana is neither an abstract, speculative topic nor a kind of guaranteed intensity. It is a discipline of selflessness and a consummation which no discipline can ever attain. As we noted earlier, few are those who arrive at the goal of the Eightfold Path. Yet the way is open to all. For to walk this road is to participate in what lies at the end. Whether we are suited to the extrovertive path of selfless service, the aesthetic realization of the oneness of reality, or the blissful loss of self in the fullness of the present, we may respond to the call of the Buddha: "Come, this is the Way, this is the course I followed. . . . You yourself must make an effort. The tathagatas (Buddhas) are only preachers. . . . Work out your own salvation with diligence!"

NOTES

1 Edward Conze, *Buddhism: Its Essence and Development* (New York: Harper Torchbooks, 1959), p. 22.

2 *Bodhicharyavatara*, trans. L. D. Barnett, as cited in E. A. Burtt, ed., *The Teachings of the Compassionate Buddha* (New York: New American Library, 1955), pp. 139–140.

3 Trans. D. T. Suzuki, as cited by Burtt, *ibid.*, pp. 165–166.

4 Ninian Smart, *The Religious Experience of Mankind* (New York: Charles Scribner's Sons, 1969), p. 181.

5 Conze, *ibid.*, p. 25.

6 Walpola Rahula, *What the Buddha Taught* (New York: Grove Press, 1962), p. 42. Copyright © 1959 by W. Rahula.

7 *Newsweek* (May 12, 1969), p. 104.

THE LEGITIMACY
OF
RELIGIOUS IRRELIGION

Part Three

THE LEGITIMACY
OF
RELIGIOUS IRRELIGION

5

<<<<<<<<<<<<<<<<<<<<<<<<<<<<<<<<<<<<<<<<<<<<<<<<<<

How to Be a Jewish Atheist

THE CRITICS OF RELIGION

THE PRESENT ERA has been described by Jawaharlal Nehru, the late prime minister of India, as "an age of disillusionment, of doubt and uncertainty. . . ." Reflecting his personal attitude toward the religions of the West as well as the religious heritage of India, he stated: "We can no longer accept many of the ancient beliefs and customs; we have no more faith in them, in Asia or in Europe or America. So we search for new ways."

A few years ago, I heard Rabbi Abraham Heschel conclude an address somewhat as follows: "George Bernard Shaw said, 'Youth is a wonderful thing. What a pity that it's wasted on the young.' And I say unto you, 'Judaism is a wonderful thing. . . .' "

I place these quotations in juxtaposition because they reflect the predicament in which religion finds itself at present. Nehru, the chief architect of modern India, expressed the sentiment of so many of today's intellectuals, activists, and reformers: "We can no longer accept . . . we have no more faith. . . ." We must find "new ways." The new ways for which they search are neither religious nor antireligious. To the Nehrus of our day, it is an insult to offer metaphysical affirmations and ceremonial observances to a starving man. Nor will the denial of beliefs and ceremonies feed him. To these hard-headed pragmatists, preoccupation with ideological issues is an obstacle to more vital tasks at hand. The human race can hardly confront the proximate issues upon which its survival depends. Why should it waste its energies on ultimate questions? East and West, in Marxist and capitalistic societies, in democracies and totalitarian states, the same sentiment is heard. Ideology—theistic or atheistic, bourgeois platitudes or Leninist maxims, chauvinistic nationalism or world-embracing universalism—is the opiate of the masses.

A new breed of this-worldly, technologically oriented managers seems ready to inherit the earth. As ubiquitous as the telephone, as interchangeable as Volkswagen parts, these technocrats and middle managers have no interest in Talmudic disputations, the Koranic doctrine of the afterlife, the Vedantic concept of liberation, the conflicts of the major Buddhist schools, or the evolution of trinitarian dogma in the early Church. Let the religious man spend an eternity probing ultimate issues. The makers and shapers of the contemporary world are content to solve *immediate* problems *immediately*. They can discuss production quotas, the expansion of vital services, the transportation of goods, the exchange rate, the training of workers, the elimination of slums, the conquest of outer space. No problem is beyond their imagination. But ask an Indian medical student about the Upanishads, or an Israeli aeronautical engineer about Hasidism, or an Austrian sociologist about Vatican II, or an American stockbroker about substitutionary atonement, and observe the expressions of consternation and chagrin.

Rabbi Heschel's remark approaches the same problem from the standpoint of the traditionally religious man. There is nothing wrong with *religion*, he implies. It is foolish to accuse *religion* of irrelevance to the contemporary situation, or of operating in a regressive fashion. The problem is not with Judaism *but with Jews*; not with Christianity *but with Christians*; not with Islam *but with Muslims*; and so on. As Harvey Cox has suggested, the greatest threat to the Church is not unbelief but hypocrisy.

Perhaps the hypocrites denounced by Heschel and Cox and one-world-at-a-time secularists represented by Nehru are the same men. Perhaps institutional religion is losing its hold on the world of mundane concerns precisely because it has been instrumental in establishing the reign of self-sufficient secularism. If there is any merit in Heschel's distinction between Judaism and Jews (and in parallel distinctions between the other religions of the world and their hypocrites), it consists in calling attention to the fact that modern man's criticism of traditional religion is more often than not modern man's criticism of himself. The danger in

Heschel's clever aphorism is that the hearer will place the fault in another's bosom. "What a shame that Judaism has been spoiled by those Jews."

The discernment of two classes of believers—the pious and the hypocritical; professors and possessors of religion; true believers and so-called believers—can degenerate into a classic cop-out. For example, when sociologists Charles Y. Glock and Rodney Stark[1] postulated a causal link between certain Christian doctrines (and degrees of commitment to Christian doctrine) and bigotry, they were widely chided by denominational spokesmen for their failure to differentiate between real Christians and those who merely called themselves Christians. Since in the eyes of the critics of the Glock-Stark survey Christian faith and bigotry are mutually exclusive, the attempt to connect Christian convictions with anti-Semitism had to be misguided. (Of course, the victims of prejudice can be just as a prioristic. Since the principal persecutors of the Jews have been Christians [who else in predominantly Christian countries?], it must be the case that Christian faith promotes hostility toward the Jews—or so it is often argued.)

As we noted earlier, a religion consists of both the manifestation and betrayal of ideals. Since such ideals are impossible by definition, their realization may never be more than approximated. Religion is based on the awareness of a gap between *is* and *ought to be*. Moreover, it is a program for overcoming the gap—gradually, progressively, and asymptotically. The impossible vision is always the elusive dream.

Otherwise it would not be worthy of man's unconditional devotion. But the real tragedy of man's religion is not the failure to realize hopeless goals, but the perversion of these goals.

As a human activity among other human activities, religion experiences the ambiguities from which all human pursuits suffer. Profane elements are present in every religious act—for religion is the awareness of the holy or divine *in, through,* and *despite* the finitude of the objects, persons, institutions, etc., which mediate its presence. As Paul Tillich noted:

> . . . the real object of honest attacks on organized religion is the ambiguity of religion in the context of the institutionalized form. Instead of transcending the finite in the direction of the infinite, institutionalized religion actually becomes a finite reality itself—a set of prescribed doctrines to be accepted, a social pressure group along with others, a political power with all the implications of power politics.[2]

Under such conditions, it is not surprising that the critics of religion are blind to its self-transcendent and holy character. But even more serious than the limited vision of religion's critics is the idolatry of religious men, that is, their commitment to the forms which mediate the presence of the divine rather than to the divine itself.

All too often, religious men have confused *religion*—the given conceptual, ethical, and ceremonial forms of a particular era—with *revelation*—the divine presence which is partially disclosed and partially obscured through these forms. Revelation—the self-disclosure of the holy—is unambiguous, but its reception is always ambiguous. Revelation is existentially distorted by the psychological, biological, and sociological factors of the actual situation *in* and *through* which it is received. No matter what its adherents may claim, there is no such thing as a "revealed religion." For religion is man's struggle with the demands of the revelator—a struggle marked by human resistance to, misunderstanding of, and only occasional harmony with the divine purpose. When the religious man ignores the glaring discrepancies between actual religion and the unconditional demands upon which religion is based, he abandons both his freedom and his responsibilities as a man. The dangerous life of dialogue with a living Presence for the purpose of redeeming the world gives way to submission to the rules, beliefs, and ceremonies of an authoritarian institution. This usurpation of the place of God by religion is the source of the unsettling foment within traditional religion at present as well as the hasty rejection of religion by so many intellectuals, social reformers, and theologians.

But the confusion of religion and revelation is not the only ambiguity threatening religion in the modern world. Much more fundamental are the ambiguities arising from the "too much of a good thing" syndrome. Every valuable function performed by religion gives birth to a parallel dysfunction. Religion enables men to face the powerlessness, frustration, and deprivation which characterize the human situation. Thomas F. O'Dea describes six functions by which religion "gives security and assurance to human beings to sustain their morale":

(1) religion, by its invocation of a beyond [i.e., a non-empirical or supraempirical order] which is concerned with human destiny and welfare, and to which men may respond and relate themselves, provides *support, consolation,* and *reconciliation.*

(2) religion offers a *transcendental relationship* through cult and the ceremonies of worship, and thereby provides the emotional ground for a new *security* and firmer *identity* amid the uncertainties and impossibilities of the human condition and the flux and change of history.

(3) religion *sacralizes the norms and values* of established society, maintaining the dominance of group goals over individual impulses. It thereby reinforces the legitimation of the division of functions, facilities, and rewards characteristic of a given society . . . thereby aiding order and stability; and . . . the reconciliation of the disaffected.

(4) religion . . . may also provide standards of value in terms of which institutionalized norms may be critically examined and found seriously wanting.

(5) religion performs important *identity* functions. . . . Individuals, by their acceptance of the values involved in

religion and the beliefs about human nature and destiny associated with them, develop important aspects of their own self-understanding and self-definition.

(6) religion is related to the growth and maturation of the individual and his passage through the various age gradings distinguished by his society.

But, as O'Dea notes, these very functions give rise to six corresponding dysfunctions:

(1) By providing support and consolation, religion may encourage apathy to actual problems and thus postpone needed reforms.

(2) By providing security and identity in a rapidly changing world, religion may cause men to ignore the current situation and seek strength from solutions of the past.

(3) By sacralizing the norms of established society, religion may legitimate injustice, exploitation, and the status quo.

(4) even though the prophetic function of religion may negate the consequences of deifying the status quo, there is always the danger that religious demands for reform will become so utopian that they will produce an anarchistic extremism.

(5) the identity provided by one's religion may impede the development of new identities more appropriate to new situations.

(6) religion may institutionalize and routinize immatur-

ity by providing the individual with answers when he needs
to grapple with fundamental issues for himself.[3]

If the contemporary critics are correct, the legitimate
functions of religion have been virtually overwhelmed by
their corresponding dysfunctions. According to reformers
within as well as enemies without, traditional religion does
little more than underwrite the inequities of the established
order, excuse bigotry, encourage class and racial divisions,
and oppose human progress. Even more powerful than the
unifying urge toward ecumenicity is the voice of the disen-
chanted faithful and their allies among the nonbelieving
—a voice which calls upon institutionalized religion to lay
down its life for the sake of mankind.

The major religions of the world are centuries removed
from the charismatic personalities, revelatory moments, redemptive events, and history-transforming situations of
their birth and youth. Power, prestige, and respectability
have long since replaced the spiritual forces which once
energized them. Like all living things, they have come to
their dotage. If they are able to survive, to once again
shape and transform men as well as civilizations, it will not
be through the pursuit of yesterday's glories. Not by following the path of institutional self-interest, of maxims and
platitudes, of ceremonies and oblations, but only by a
radical coming to terms with the present can religion hope
to serve the man of today.

I am not suggesting the deification of the present advocated by our current neo-Bonhoefferians. We are not living in the golden age—why should we force our ideals and aspirations to conform with the present? We are living in an era of dehumanization, of moral and aesthetic devaluation, of irrational violence, of unbelievable contrasts between the affluent few and the deprived many. Man has not come of age; he has not learned to do without God. No! What is really so terrifying and at the same time so hilarious is that *God is not dead.* To the vast majority of Americans and to hundreds of millions of others, *the God of traditional faith is very much alive as the creator, sustainer, and guarantor of the present age.* And since such a God is an idol, a diabolic counterfeit, it would appear that atheism and irreligion are the most appropriate *religious* responses. For when God is the reification of the status quo and religion functions chiefly as the chaplaincy of the Establishment, men who strive after the unrealized *ought* in the face of the inadequate *is* must oppose and resist both God and religion.

But the rejection of the traditions of the fathers is not without regrets. I am not speaking of the immature rejection of immature religion, the empty cynicism that discards what it never really possessed. What I have in mind is the sorrowful departure from one's childhood religion in the name of the God who transcends and judges all religion. I am thinking of those who have become spiritually homeless and rootless for the sake of values which the religion of their fathers betrayed, corrupted, and destroyed. Even if such rejection is rash and immoderate, the source of its passion is profoundly religious.

THE POET-PROPHETS OF RELIGIOUS IRRELIGION

The principal spokesmen for such religious irreligion have been novelists and poets rather than theologians or social activists. The "poet-prophet"—if we may give a general name to this class— may be a Jew (Leonard Cohen), a Protestant (John Updike), a Catholic (Wilfred Sheed), or a Hindu (Rabindranath Tagore). But whatever his background, he is motivated by nostalgia for the God of the fathers but outraged by the religion of his contemporaries. There is a moving example in Leonard Cohen's semi-autobiographical novel, *The Favorite Game*. As he prepares to leave his boyhood Montreal, Lawrence Breavman reflects upon his family's participation in the Sabbath services:

He had thought that his tall uncles in their dark clothes were princes of an elite brotherhood. He had thought the synagogue was their house of purification. He had thought their businesses were realms of feudal benevolence. But he had grown to understand that none of them even pretended to these things. They were proud of their financial and communal success. They liked to be first, to be respected, to sit close to the altar, to be called up to lift the scrolls. They weren't pledged to any other idea. They did not believe their blood was consecrated. Where had he got the notion that they did?

When he saw the rabbi and cantor move in their white robes, the light on the brocaded letters of their prayer shawls; when he stood among his uncles and bowed with them and joined his voice to theirs in the responses; when he followed in the prayer book the catalogue of magnificence. . . .

No, his uncles were not grave enough. They were strict, not grave. They did not seem to realize how fragile the ceremony was. They participated in it blindly, as if it would last forever. They did not seem to realize how important they were, not self-important, but important to the incantation, the altar, the ritual. They were ignorant of the craft of devotion. They were merely devoted. They never thought how close the ceremony was to chaos. Their nobility was insecure because it rested on inheritance and not moment-to-moment creation in the face of annihilation.

In the most solemn or joyous part of the ritual Breavman knew the whole procedure would revert in a second to desolation. The cantor, the rabbi, the chosen laymen stood before the open Ark, cradling the Torah scrolls, which looked like stiff-necked royal children, and returned them one by one to their golden stall. The beautiful melody soared which proclaimed that the Law was a tree of life and a path of peace. Couldn't they see how it had to be nourished? And all these men who bowed, who performed the customary motions, they were unaware that other men had written the sacred tune, other men had developed the seemingly eternal gestures out of clumsy confusion. They took for granted what was dying in their hands.

But why should he care? He wasn't Isaiah, and the people claimed nothing. He didn't even like the people or the god of their cult. He had no rights in the matter.

He didn't want to blame anyone. Why should he feel that they had bred him to a disappointment? He was bitter because he couldn't inherit the glory they unwittingly advertised. He couldn't be part of their brotherhood but he wanted to be among them. A nostalgia for solidarity. . . .⁴

Cohen describes a religiosity which imitates the past without renewing it. Ceremonies which once expressed a sense of peoplehood, of divine election, of covenant responsibilities, of meaning amidst suffering, have been transformed into celebrations of financial success and personal achievement. The New World Jew, like his counterparts the immigrant Catholic and the Protestant pioneer, has allowed his traditional religion to become perverted by what William James termed "our national disease": the worship of success. As Norman Podhoretz observes in his remarkable literary memoir, *Making It*:

The immigrant Jewish milieu from which I derive is by now fixed for all time in the American imagination as having been driven by an uninhibited hunger for success. This reputation is by no means justified as we have been led to believe, but certainly on the surface the "gospel of success" did reign supreme in the world of my childhood. Success did not necessarily, or even primarily, mean money; just as often it might mean prestige or popularity. . . . The main thing was to be esteemed. . . .[5]

The Jewish poet-prophets are the children (in some instances grandchildren) of Eastern European immigrants who themselves had been reared in scrupulously orthodox homes. But success in the new environment meant accommodation of tradition to the American situation. Without the reinforcement of the exclusively Jewish ghetto or *stetl* (village), the Jew assimilated to the American way and its value structure as much as he was allowed. Yet even where it was not forced upon him, he still retained a sense of Jewish identity. This consciousness of Jewishness, born of the identity crisis he felt in the American melting pot, his reverence for the past, and his uneasiness about the future, came to replace the practice of Judaism as the *sine qua non* of Jewish existence in the New World. "Out of a commitment to Jewish survival that was more instinctual than reasoned" (Podhoretz), the immigrant vowed that his children would be Jews, receive Jewish education, and succeed in careers respected by non-Jews and Jews alike. But this last proviso—that his children succeed—meant that his sons and daughters would be Americans first and Jews second.

To be an American first and a Jew second meant that one received his elementary and secondary education in public school while devoting late afternoons to his "Jewish education"—preparation for bar mitzvah, elements of Hebrew, snatches of the Talmud, patches of Jewish history. To be an American first and a Jew second meant that one attended the best (preferably Ivy League) college possible without wholly renouncing his Jewishness. Thus, a generation of Jewish intellectuals came into being and flourished in America.

In a sense, their intellectualism was part and parcel of the Jewish past. During the period of their segregation from the mainstream of European life, the Jews had learned that the only secure capital is that which it carried in their brains. Before the Napoleonic era, European Jewry was forbidden to own land, vote, attend the universities, hold civil posts, or enter the professions. Cut off from most careers, forced into the ghettoes, Jews directed their talents in the only directions open to them—trade and study. Jewish success in commerce demonstrated how well ingenuity and common sense could compensate for material deprivations. (It also gave rise to pathological stereotypes which have plagued the Jew to this very day.)

But the capitalization of brainpower which was most esteemed by the Jews themselves was the study and exposition of Jewish tradition. A people threatened with extermination, surrounded by enemies, incessantly victimized by brutal neighbors, turned in desperation to the custodians of their heritage to understand who they were and why they suffered. The sage—the saintly interpreter of the Law—

was revered as a prince. Neither the rich nor the powerful enjoyed such respect.

Thus, when the ghetto walls fell before the egalitarian tide which swept Europe in the nineteenth century, Jewish respect for scholarship provided the motivation (just as Jewish success in commerce supplied the means) for entrance into law, medicine, the civil service, education, and letters. But the new world of intellectual opportunity was also quicksand to the Jewish soul. For Jewishness—whether it was defined in religious, social, or cultural terms—proved an impediment to realization of the universal community of gentlemen and scholars. Hence, the Jewish intellectual forgot his Jewishness, ignored his heritage, and enjoyed his success. But two forces were at work which would rudely interrupt his contentment. The first was the systematic destruction of European Jewry by the machinery of the Third Reich. The second was an inner uneasiness, anxiety, and rootlessness which grew ever more profound, despite all that had been achieved.

A renewed sense of Jewish solidarity sprang from "Hitler's altogether irrefutable demonstration of the inescapability of Jewishness . . ." (Podhoretz). Terror, disbelief, and indignation were the first response as the record of genocide became public. Responsibility was (and for many Jews remains) the chief issue. Various scapegoats were produced: Christian anti-Semitism, the apathy of Pope Pius XII, the intrinsic barbarism of the German nation, and, above all, the passivity of the victims. Listen to the rage of Leonard

Cohen as he attributes Jewish suffering to Jewish faith in "Absurd Prayer":

> I disdain God's suffering. . . .
> Men command sufficient pain.
> I'll keep to my tomb
> Though the Messiah come.
>
> Though He summon every corpse
> To throng the final Throne,
> One heap shall remain
> Immovable as stone.
>
> The ruins of men and women
> Resume their hair and skin
> And straightway to the altar-steps
> In trembling fear they run.
>
> They wallow in His Glory,
> They scramble for His Hem.
> These bodies rose from Paradise
> But they kneel down in Doom.
>
> Hyenas wait beyond the steps.
> I sight them from this hole.
> Their appetites are whetted,
> They feed on carrion soul.[6]

Much as the Black Nationalist has come to despise the Christian faith which comforted his ancestors and thus allowed them to be exploited, so many of the Jewish poet-prophets fumed and fulminated as they thought of millions of Jews shuffling into the gas chambers with the praise of

God on their lips. Was it for this that God had chosen us, to be

> ... a Dachau jew
> and lie down in lime
> with twisted limbs
> and bloated pain
> no mind can understand?[7]

Hitler's reminder of their irrefutable Jewishness provoked an ineludible crisis of identity. The self-hatred evident in the condemnation of Jewish faith was no answer. Ineluctably, almost against its will, the Jewish intellectual community underwent a conversion from self-transcendence to self-affirmation. As Podhoretz observes:

> Marxism, the creation of a baptized German Jew, issues the command: "Transcend yourself and join in the universal struggle to bring about the self-transcendence of all men!" Psychoanalysis, the creation of an acculturated German Jew who never underwent baptism, demands by contrast: "Accept yourself for what you are and make use of it!" It is accordingly no accident, as disciples of both schools of thought once liked to say, that Jews have been among the most eager listeners to these calls, many of them responding first to one and then to the other at different periods of their lives. Thus it was with the second generation [of American Jewish writers]: from Marx to Freud, from self-transcendence to self-acceptance. Schwartz, Bellow, Rosenfeld, Kazin, Fiedler, and Howe—products

every one of Yiddish-speaking households—all proclaimed their Jewishness, took relish in it, wrote stories, poems, and articles about it; and so, at the same time did several members of the first generation, like Rosenberg and Goodman, begin to do. Of course, more was involved here than the influence of Freud: Hitler's altogether irrefutable demonstration of the inescapability of Jewishness was no doubt an even more important factor in the emergence of this new attitude."[8]

The culmination of this process are such semi-autobiographical statements as Cohen's *The Favorite Game* and Phillip Roth's *Portnoy's Complaint*. Both works are "confessions" (in the classic form of St. Augustine's spiritual memoirs) of less than successful assimilation. Both heroes, Lawrence Breavman and Alex Portnoy, are products of Jewish homes which are not only *typical* but *archetypal*. Breavman and Portnoy are so *déraciné* that they are unable to pronounce a single Jewish word with confidence. Both have broken with Jewish religion and tradition. For Portnoy, the rejection of Judaism was an act of "adolescent resentment and Oedipal rage" directed by a rebellious fourteen-year-old at his father. For Breavman, it is a brokenhearted realization that the empty, societal religion of his industrialist uncles cannot deliver what it promises.

Even though Breavman and Portnoy enjoy the forbidden fruits of assimilation—sexual conquest and professional success—neither is able to shake his residual Jewishness. In Portnoy's case, his inescapable Jewishness is the basis of his "complaint," which Roth defines as "A disorder in which strongly felt ethical and altruistic impulses are perpetually warring with extreme sexual longings, often of a perverse nature."

Breavman chastises all religion, declaring in his jeremiad for Montreal:

> A religious stink hovers above this city and we all breathe it. Work goes on at the Oratoire St. Joseph, the copper is raised. The Temple Emmanuel initiates a building fund. A religious stink composed of musty shrine and tabernacle smells, decayed wreaths and rotting bar-mitzvah tables. Boredom, money, vanity, guilt, packs the pews. The candles, memorials, eternal lights shine unconvincingly, like neon signs, sincere as advertising. The holy vessels belch miasmal smoke. Good lovers turn away.[9]

And, yet, it is the same young, self-proclaimed enemy of religion who ponders over a summer camp worship service:

> Friday night. Sabbath. Ritual music on the PA. Holy, holy, holy, Lord God of Hosts. The earth is full of your glory. If I could only end my hate. If I could believe what they wrote and wrapped in silk and crowned with gold. I want to write the word.
>
> All our bodies are brown. All the children are dressed in white. Make us able to worship.
>
> Take me home again. Build up my house again. Make me

a dweller in thee. Take away my pain. I can't use it any
longer. It makes nothing beautiful. It makes the leaves into
cinders. It makes the water foul. It makes your body into
a stone. Holy life. Let me lead it. I don't want to hate. Let
me flourish. Let the dream of you flourish in me.[10]

Breavman represents an entire generation which abhors
Jewishness while yearning for Zion; which loathes the
stereotyped Jewish culture of the Diaspora while seeking a
personal role in the rebirth of the Jewish people. For such
Jews the re-creation of the State of Israel in 1948 was the
beginning of a new chapter in Jewish history, the basis for a
deeply satisfying participation in Jewish destiny. Since the
time of their unsuccessful rebellion against their Roman
masters, the Jews had been at the mercy of Gentile caprice.
For nearly two thousand years, they had been forced to
bear the humiliations of political and social impotence.
But the establishment of a Jewish state as the result of the
United Nations' partition of Palestine ended the era of
weakness and shame. The present generation of Jews has
leaped back in time to the days of heroism depicted in the
Bible.

To the Zionist elite dedicated to the preservation of Israel and the enhancement of Jewish life, the religious culture of the ghettoes of Europe is a painful reminder of an
ignominy which is best forgotten. Since the borscht-circuit
Yiddishkeit of American Jewry retains and glorifies the

Diaspora, there is a fundamental gap between Israel and American Jewish culture. As a result, it is most difficult for a Jew to be religious—according to an American Jewish conception of religion—in Israel.

Harold R. Isaacs states that during his own visit to Jerusalem:

> . . . I heard an American student report on one of his own experiments in a mixed Israeli-American class with lists of paired qualities to be attributed to "Israelis" or "Jews." He reported with some indignant dismay that the Israeli students in the class tended to assign the most favorable qualities in a lopsided way to the "Israeli" (who was seen as clean, progressive, a man of action, tall, aggressive, self-respecting, self-confident, strong, free) and to ascribe a much greater share of the opposite negative attributes to "Jew" (dirty, regressive, man of words, short, defensive, lacking self-respect, lacking in self-confidence, weak, constrained).[11]

What a bitter irony that the very stereotypes employed by the Nazi propaganda machine to justify genocide should reappear in Jewish minds. As long as American Jewry rests content in its comfortable security, sated by the fruits of our capitalistic economy, it will be despised by young Sabras (native born Israelis).

It is difficult for the American Jew to understand the attitude of the Sabra. Where, asks the American, is the gratitude owed by Israel to the American Jewish community for the financial, moral, and political support which made the birth and survival of Israel possible? The Israeli replies that American Jewry should remember that what happened in Germany can happen anywhere. As long as Jewish fate is in non-Jewish hands, it is in deadly peril. It may turn out that the American Jew had done himself rather than the Israeli a great favor by contributing to the establishment of the ultimate refuge for beleaguered Jews. What is more, can Israel's friends claim special thanks for doing what is morally obligatory? Could the conscience of American Jewry bear the destruction of Israel?

But not only does the Zionist elite spurn the Jewishness of his American cousin, he ruthlessly attacks his religion as well. In America, the individual indicates his self-identification with the Jewish experience through synagogue affiliation. Membership in a place of worship and community activity is regarded by Jews as well as non-Jews as the sign of one's intention to remain Jewish despite the assimilative pressures of the American way of life. Further, the binding of one's person and fortune to a Jewish house of prayer and study provides a defense against the loss of one's children. The growth of institutional religion among Jewish Americans is governed by a basic law: Synagogues proliferate in direct proportion to the rate of religious and racial intermarriage.

But in Israel the antiassimilation functions of Jewish religion would be superfluous. As Portnoy discovers when fate casts him on Israeli shores: "I am in a Jewish country.

In this country, everybody is Jewish." And although it may sound preposterous, it is necessary to ask, what does it mean to be a Jew in a place where everybody is Jewish? The all-Jewish character of the State of Israel has forced a horrendous identity problem upon Judaism.

To the American Jew, religion is an essential part of being Jewish. No matter how far he strays from the ceremonial and cultic requirements of Jewish religion, the American Jew's feeling of Jewishness is firmly rooted in his acceptance of or reaction to Judaism. But in Israel the situation is radically different. In the first place, *to be religious is to be Orthodox or to be nothing*. The Rabbinic or Halachic legalism of the European ghettoes, the Talmudic code of behavior which is observed by only a minority of Israelis, totally dominates the State of Israel. Through a shrewd use of their power in the coalition politics of Israel, approximately fifteen percent of the population is able to suppress all forms of Judaism other than their own and to paralyze the nation when their privileged status is threatened.

No one may be married or buried without the approval of the Orthodox. Thousands of Israelis are considered illegitimate because their parents were not wed under Orthodox auspices. Rita Eitani, a heroine in the struggle for the establishment of Israel, was stripped of her citizenship and threatened with deportation due to her opposition to the religious authorities. Mrs. Eitani was forced to undergo ritual conversion to Judaism in order to regain her citizenship and legitimize her marriage and her children. Such repression in the name of religion has only served to stiffen the resistance of the young to all religion. The youthful zealots stake all of their hopes for the future of the Jewish people on the re-creation of a Jewish nation. They regard the Orthodox establishment as part of an unfortunate heritage, a relic of a despised past. Only the common peril unites religious, irreligious, and apathetic. When the Arab threat subsides, Israel will be rent with dissension as long-sublimated resentments are aired. This long-avoided showdown may be decisive for the future of Judaism.

The Jewish poet-prophets represent a chic, fashionable Jewishness. But their self-affirmation is more "complaint" than celebration. For at the very core of the stylish new Jewishness is a God-sized void. Perhaps this is the protojoke upon which all Jewish humor is based, the final irony at which we can only laugh because we can do nothing but laugh. I will never forget a lovely eighteen-year-old freshman who expressed this irony so aptly (and without intention). "I do not believe in G-d," she wrote in a blue book. "The author is obviously a *Jewish* atheist," I thought.

I must close this chapter with a dilemma—an unfathomable quandary which confronts every sensitive soul, Christian as well as Jew, Oriental as well as Occidental, traditionalist as well as antireligious. At a time when "God" symbolizes only the dysfunctions and disvalues of institutionalized religion, when nothing but noise is heard in the solemn assemblies, how is it possible not to be an atheist? And, yet, if the altruistic urges refuse to leave the psyche, if the desperate longing after one's place in the people of God refuses to be stilled, if the hound of heaven persists despite every folly, rationalization, and denial—what then must a man do in order to be a *Jewish* atheist?

NOTES

[1] Charles Y. Glock and Rodney Stark, *Christian Beliefs and Anti-Semitism* (New York: Harper and Row, 1966).

[2] Paul Tillich, *Future of Religions*, ed. Jerald C. Brauer (New York: Harper and Row, 1966), p. 99.

[3] Condensed from Thomas F. O'Dea, *The Sociology of Religion* (Englewood Cliffs, N.J.: Prentice-Hall, 1966), pp. 14–15. © 1966. Reprinted by permission of Prentice-Hall, Inc., Englewood Cliffs, New Jersey.

[4] Leonard Cohen, *The Favorite Game* (New York: Avon Books, 1965), pp. 103–104. Copyright © 1963 by Leonard Cohen; all rights reserved; reprinted by permission of The Viking Press, Inc.

[5] Norman Podhoretz, *Making It* (New York: Bantam Books, 1969), p. 11.

[6] Leonard Cohen, *Spice-Box of Earth* (New York: Bantam Books, 1968), p. 71. Originally published as "Absurd Prayer," from *Selected Poems, 1956–1968*, by Leonard Cohen. Copyright in all countries of the International Copyright Union. All rights reserved. Reprinted by permission of the Viking Press, Inc.

[7] "The Genius," *ibid.*, p. 76.

[8] Podhoretz, *op. cit.*, p. 92.

[9] *The Favorite Game*, p. 184.

[10] *Ibid.*, p. 171.

[11] Harold R. Isaacs, *American Jews in Israel* (New York: John Day, 1966), p. 141.

6

The Religious Irreligion of Rabindranath Tagore

THE INDIAN RENAISSANCE

WHEN THE BRITISH granted independence to India in 1948, the domination of a third of a billion Hindus by rulers of other faiths was at long last ended. For the first time in centuries the destiny of Hinduism rested in Hindu hands. Gone with the British government was the universal inferiority complex which had afflicted Hinduism during the successive reigns of the Mughals, who had controlled India during the Islamic golden age, and the various European colonists—the Dutch, the French, the Portuguese, the Danish, and, above all, the British—who had sent flag and Bible in the wake of commerce.

Independence meant much more than the fulfillment of the nationalistic hopes that had involved hundreds of thousands in decades of political agitation. Of profounder significance to the Indian psyche was the resurgence of

Hindu civilization, the rebirth of a distinctively Hindu society and culture based upon the heritage of the past but directed to the circumstances of the present. Political independence was one of a series of stepping stones in a slow process of Hindu reformation which began during British rule and which continues today.

Scholars are fond of comparing the Indian Renaissance with the European. The European Renaissance owed its origins to an alien mentality (Islam) and a dead culture (Hellenism). As C. F. Andrews observed: ". . . it was the shock of Arab civilization and the faith of Islam which startled the West out of the intellectual torpor of the Dark Ages. Then followed the recovery [via the Arabs] of the Greek and Latin Classics."[1] The consequences of the European Renaissance were, in the words of an Indian writer:

> a lessening of the hold of religion on man, an increased interest in terrestrial affairs and especially in man, a love of freedom and adventure, and extension of the empire of reason, a contraction of the sway of superstition, a greater preoccupation with literature and art, a revision of values of life—in short, a fresh play of the human spirit and an enrichment of the human personality.[2]

Like the European Renaissance, the rebirth of Hinduism was the result of the shock of an alien civilization. But whereas the European Renaissance represents the death of the religious theonomy of medieval life, the Indian Renaissance is firmly rooted in Hindu tradition. The Indian

Renaissance was the result of two forces: (a) the impact upon India of western technology, political structures, religious institutions, and ideological pragmatism; and (b) the revival of the Sanskrit classics and the reformation of religious Hinduism.

The forces meet in the literary and artistic renewal of the nineteenth and early twentieth century in Bengal. At the beginning of the nineteenth century, the burning question in Bengal was whether the spread of English should be encouraged or not. In a famous minute, written in 1835, Thomas Babington Macaulay, member of the Supreme Council of India, fixed English as the medium for higher education, basing his case on the alleged uselessness of both the Sanskrit classics (Hinduism's scriptures) and Bengali literature. In reaction to the attempted westernization of language and culture, there was a great shaking of Indian religious and social foundations.

The outstanding personality of this time of indigenous revival was Ram Mohun Roy (1774–1833). While enthusiastically supporting Macaulay's proposal and ardently promoting the new western learning, Ram Mohun sought at the same time to recreate in Bengali hearts a reverence for the Indian past which would lead to a revival of the Sanskrit classics. His own literary pursuits brought Bengali back into full use. In addition, he crusaded for the reform of Hindu customs. Through his efforts, the self-immolation of widows upon their husbands' funeral pyres was outlawed in 1829.

Almost as important as Ram Mohun Roy was Debendranath Tagore. Known universally as the "Maharishi" (Great Seer), Tagore took over the leadership of the liberal religious association which Ram Mohun had founded. The earlier society had been a meeting place for all men without distinction for the worship of the One True God, without the use of any images or sectarian ritual. Under Tagore's direction, the Brahmo Samaj became a theistic association which revered the Hindu Upanishads, together with the scriptures of other religions, and which met for prayer and study. Always more of an intellectual discussion group than a religious sect, the Brahmo Samaj was responsible for a number of social reforms. The Samaj's attempt to synthesize Hinduism with the social activism of western ethical theism had an undeniable impact upon all contemporary Hindu leaders. But its overeagerness to transform Hinduism into a kind of "Indian Ethical Culture Society" alienated the majority of Hindus. Rent by dissent and supported only by an educated elite, the influence of the Samaj soon receded.

RABINDRANATH TAGORE

Rabindranath Tagore, the seventh son of the revered Brahmo Samaj leader, was born in Calcutta, May 6, 1861. If any one man was symbolic of the Indian Renaissance, it was Rabindranath. Second only to Gandhi in the esteem of his countrymen, Tagore would turn western attention to Indian literature and religion, becoming the first Asian to win the Nobel Prize for literature. Tagore was born into a family which was earnestly attempting to discover the meaning of the Hindu scriptures in the light of India's modern situation, particularly her exposure to western technology and religion.

But for young Tagore, the Brahmo Samaj synthesis of ethical monotheism and Upanishadic philosophy was a cold, pale abstraction. Consciously, he rejected the religion of his elders. After his investiture with the sacred thread at the age of twelve, he was taken for a long stay with his father in the Himalayas. This was their first intimate contact. Rabindranath gratefully reported: "As he allowed me to wander about the mountains at my will, so in the quest of truth he left me free to select my path. He was not deterred by the danger of my making mistakes, he was not alarmed at the prospect of my encountering sorrow. He held up a standard, not a disciplinary rod."[3] The young Tagore remained "coolly aloof, absolutely uninfluenced by any religion whatever."[4]

Unconsciously, he followed the path of his Indian ancestors. From his earliest days Rabindranath felt a deep love for nature—a love which first broke forth into verse when he was eight. In the varied phenomena of nature his mind was held with the intimacy of pervasive companionship. At his initiation the *gayatri* verse given to him ran, "Let me contemplate the adorable splendour of him who created the earth, the air and the starry spheres, and sends the power of comprehension within our minds." There was born in him a vague but persuasive sense of an infinite harmony which underlies the creative mind of the poet and the natural world.

It was when Tagore was eighteen that "a sudden spring breeze of religious experience for the first time came. . . ."[5] As he recalled this moment of personal revelation:

> One morning I happened to be standing on the verandah. . . . The sun was just rising through the leafy tops of those trees. As I continued to gaze, all of a sudden a covering seemed to fall away from my eyes, and I found the world bathed in a wonderful radiance, with waves of beauty and joy swelling on every side.[6]

> I suddenly felt as if some ancient mist had in a moment lifted from my sight, and the morning light on the face of the world revealed an inner radiance of joy. The invisible screen of the commonplace was removed from all things and all men, their ultimate significance was intensified in my mind.[7]

After four days the vision faded. The world resumed "its disguise of the obscurity of an ordinary fact." But again and again throughout his life the veil was rent by the sudden awareness of the awesome depths and transcendent meaning of the mundane. To Tagore's poetic imagination, such moments were revelatory. Thus he sings: "The same stream of life that runs through my veins night and day runs through the world and dances in rhythmic measures."[8]

Without conscious intention, Tagore had discovered the truth of the Hindu scriptures that the Universal Spirit and the human spirit are essentially one, that the divine is immanent in the natural order. But to Tagore this discovery was more than a doctrine. It was a living experience, a personal transformation.

"I felt sure," he professed, "that some Being who comprehended me and my world was seeking his best expression in all my experiences, uniting them in an ever-widening individuality which is a spiritual work of art."[9] He had entered a *creative comradeship:*

> To this Being I was responsible; for the creation in me is his as well as mine. It may be that it was the same creative Mind that is shaping the universe to its eternal idea; but in me as a person it had one of its special centres of a personal relationship growing into a deepening consciousness. . . . I felt that I had found my religion at last, the religion of Man, in which the infinite became defined in humanity and came close to me so as to need my love and cooperation.[10]

According to Tagore's vision, the same spirit which appears as the inspiration of his poetry is the source of all truth, beauty, and joy. In every man, he testifies, there is the underground current of a perennial stream which from time to time wells up to the surface. These sudden outbursts from within, whether they take the form of aesthetic production or religious expression, are manifestations of man's essential partnership with the divine.

The essence of religion, Tagore declares, is the awareness of the essential harmony of all things—a harmony which illuminates the mind and delights the senses. By actualizing his unique potentialities, by fully developing all his creative gifts, the individual contributes to the completion of the totality of beings: the realization that each person is part of an organic whole which both sustains him and depends upon his contribution. But this awareness of cosmic harmony is not merely an intellectual truth. It is a vital experience.

In each moment of living, the individual is called upon to enter into partnership, to respond with the fullness of his being. When he was alert to the divine summons, Tagore found that "This world was living to me, intimately close to my life, permeated by a subtle touch of kinship which enhanced the value of my own being."[11] During such times of sensitive openness, all relationships were charged with significance. Tagore illustrates as follows: A doctor may stand in two rather different relationships to his son. In one, he regards him from a scientific standpoint as a living organism with its physiological functions. Only by discarding his intimate feeling for his child is he able to maintain his attitude. But such objectivity obstructs the ultimate truth about his son, the truth which only personal involvement and concerned love can reveal.

The love and joy of relationship are the key to Truth itself. For our love and joy mirror "the Supreme One, who relates all things, comprehends the universe, is all love—the love that is the highest truth, being the most perfect relationship."[12] When a man stands in a true relationship to his fellowman or to the world of nature, a creative comradeship is established through which the individual shares in the ongoing work of the divine workman. It is this intuitively felt unity of the efforts of finite selves and the transcendent Self which is the wellspring of all truth, beauty, justice, and joy.

THE MYSTICAL POET

Tagore's realization of the presence of the divine Spirit at the depths of all finite beings made him a *mystical poet.* He was a *mystic* in the sense that his life's work was based on a consciousness of the fundamental unity of reality. And yet, unlike many mystics, his vision produced a radical dissatisfaction with the world as it is and a passionate determination to transform it. If relationship, responsibility, and love were the essence of Truth, then all that obstruct them must be removed. Thus, Tagore condemned the aggressive nationalism of the West as the war clouds gathered in the 1930's. He labored steadfastly for international cooperation, founding the University of Visvabharati at Santiniketan in his native Bengal. At Visvabharati, Eastern and Western scholars came together in an atmosphere where labor was considered joyous, where truth was regarded valuable not only for its own sake but as the necessary instrument for the reformation of society.

Despite a remarkably successful career as dramatist, novelist, actor, composer, educator, philosopher, lecturer, and painter, Tagore was a poet, first and foremost. According to Tagore, poetry is more than craft. It is worship, for personal creativity taps the vital energies by which the Divine Artist creates the universe. The creative individual does not produce his artifacts through his own genius, but by imitation of or participation in the work of God.

Tagore's sense of unity with a Being who calls man to partnership in all spheres of his existence expresses itself in both devotional mysticism and nature mysticism. The former is paramount in Tagore's songs of the mutual love of God and man. An especially beautiful series is found in his Nobel-Prize-winning collection, *Gitanjali*. Poems 41 to 59 describe the love shared by God and the human soul under the image of a king courting a shepherd girl. The poverty-stricken girl lives in daily hope of the coming of her beloved. Finally he passes by and is captivated by her simple songs of love. The majestic chariot stops, and the king approaches. Enigmatically, he extends his hand to ask the beggar, "What has thou to give me?" Taking what little the girl possesses, the king departs. But soon he returns to repay her surrender with his own. As Tagore poignantly paints the final scene, the girl muses:

I thought I should ask of thee—but I dared not—the rose
wreath thou hadst on thy neck. Thus I waited for the
morning, when thou didst depart, to find a few fragments
on the bed. And like a beggar I searched in the dawn
only for a stray petal or two.

Ah me, what is it I find? What token of thy love? It is no
flower, no spices, no vase of perfumed water. It is thy
mighty sword. . . .[13]

For without pain and death there can be neither love nor
joy.

More than any other contemporary religious thinker,
Tagore emphasizes the reciprocity of divine and human
love. God's love requires man's response for its completion.
The dignity and necessity of man is expressed in a song by
an uneducated Indian which Tagore was fond of quoting:

> My longing is to meet you in play of love, Lover;
> But this longing is not only mine, but also yours.
> For your lips can have their smile, and your flute
> its music, only in your delight of my love;
> and therefore you are importunate, even as I am.[14]

Adopting a philosophical motif, Tagore explains:

> The Infinite for its self-expression comes down into the
> manifoldness of the Finite; and the Finite for its self-
> realisation must rise into the unity of the Infinite. Then
> only is the cycle of Truth complete.[15]

Many parallels to Tagore's devotional poetry exist in the lyrics of Hindu piety, particularly the popular hymns to Vishnu and Krishna. But Tagore breaks with ordinary Hindu piety in two respects: (1) He discards all mythological symbols and sectarian forms in favor of universal images. D. S. Sarma observes that Tagore "speaks of God as king, master, friend, father, poet, bridegroom and lover, and not as any mythological deity or Avatar."[16] The popularity of *Gitanjali* was due in large measure to the absence of allusions to Hindu myth and its dependence upon such familiar phenomena as children at play, lovers meeting, and the rhythms of the sea. (2) Tagore does not believe that devotion requires renunciation of the world. He rejects ascetic quietism as well as every official, formalized, or institutional religion. The fervor of his "irreligion" is equal to that of the Jewish poet-prophets examined earlier. Tagore could be savage in his criticism of Hinduism. He loathed the inequities of caste, the cruel social customs (e.g., child marriage), and the apathetic fatalism which traditional religion encourages in India. But even more passionate was his condemnation of the fundamental error of distinguishing sacred and profane, religious concerns from secular interests. "Leave this chanting and singing and telling of beads," instructs the poet.

Whom dost thou worship in this lonely corner of a temple with doors all shut? open thine eyes and see thy God is not before thee!

He is there where the tiller is tilling the hard ground and where the pathmaker is breaking stones. He is with them in sun and in shower, and his garment is covered with dust. Put off thy holy mantle and even like him come down on the dusty soil.

Deliverance? Where is this deliverance to be found? Our master himself has joyfully taken upon him the bonds of creation; he is bound with us all for ever.

Come out of thy meditations and leave aside thy flowers and incense! What harm is there if thy clothes become tattered and stained? Meet him and stand by him in toil and in sweat of thy brow.[17]

God does not require that man renounce the joys and sorrows of everyday life. Indeed the divine Spirit is inextricably involved in them. Where can God be met if not in man's daily experience? Where can he be served if not in man's usual work? For only by transforming the mundane and habitual can man participate in the divine creativity. To renounce the world of the everyday, the delights of the senses, is to remove oneself from the divine-human comradeship. Tagore sings:

Today heaven lives in my body, in my love, in the anxiety of my heart, in my timidity and my strivings, my joys and sorrows.

Today heaven sings in my song and has found its fulfillment in my life.[18]

Deliverance is not for me in renunciation. I feel the
embrace of freedom in a thousand bonds of delight.

No, I will never shut the doors of my senses. The delights
of sight and hearing and touch will bear thy delight.

Yes, all my illusions will burn into illumination of joy, and
all my desires ripen into fruits of love.[19]

The consciousness of the divine presence in all things
is the source of Tagore's most distinctive contribution to
devotional literature, his nature mysticism. According to
D. S. Sarma, Tagore "breaks what is practically new ground
in [Hindu] religious literature. For in modern times we have
had no conspicuous instances of intense religious feeling
arising out of love of Nature."[20] In the classic Hindu scriptures this feeling appears only as a hardened doctrine, the
concept of divine immanence. No Hindu poet has combined such passionate love for nature with such sensitive
awareness of the divine Presence behind the phenomena
of nature.

As we have noted, in Tagore's writings the Upanishadic
doctrine of the absolute identity of the spirit in man with
the Spirit of the Universe is more than a tradition. It is a
living experience. As he reflects in a letter:

I feel as if dim, distant memories come to me of the time
when I was one with the rest of the earth; when on me
grew green grass and on me fell the autumn light; when a

warm scent of youth would rise from every pore of my vast, soft, green body at the touch of the rays of the mellow sun, and a fresh life, a sweet joy would be half-consciously secreted and inarticulately poured forth from all the immensity of my being. . . . My feelings seem to be those of the ancient earth in the daily ecstasy of its un-kissed life; *my own consciousness seems to stream through each blade of grass*, each sucking root, to rise with the sap through the trees, to break out with joyous thrills in the waving fields of corn, in the rustling palm-leaves.[21]

It should be evident that any distinction between Tagore's devotional mysticism and his nature mysticism is tenuous. For it is in and through nature—nature understood in its broadest sense to include all sentient beings as well as the inanimate forms which nourish and sustain them—that the poet encountered, responded to, and adored the object of his devotion.

For true religion is the vision of a perfect harmony of relationship—a relationship which cannot be discovered by knowledge but only by sympathy, love, and joy. This harmony reveals itself in ever-deepening relations of love for all aspects of reality, the natural, the spiritual, and the point of intersection of natural and spiritual—the personal. Peace, love, and joy are the signs of unity attained, of the reconciliation of tragic divisions. But when a man's sense of self-importance causes him to act for his own good at the cost of another's, a wall of isolation springs up which imprisons the self in its finitude. Tagore declares:

He whom I enclose with my name is weeping in this dungeon. I am ever busy building this wall all around; and as this wall goes up into the sky day by day I lose sight of my true being in its dark shadow.

I take pride in this great wall, and I plaster it with dust and sand lest a least hole be left in this name; and for all the care I take I lose sight of my true being.[22]

In the vision of Rabindranath Tagore, the search for one's true being is also the quest for authentic community. For a man can find a life worthy of his dignity as a man only through cooperation with his fellows. But the quest for community does not end with the transcending of social, national, and ideological differences. The fulfillment of man's essential humanity depends not only on harmony among men but even more basically upon a creative union of man and his environment. Unless we cease the selfish exploitation of our natural resources, unless we proscribe the mindless rape of nature for profit, we will soon destroy nature's ability to replenish and sustain life. If we continue to manipulate and lay waste, we will guarantee for our descendants a world devoid of beauty and awe.

The man who heedlessly exploits nature will heedlessly exploit his fellowman. The primary lesson of Tagore's life and work is that nature moves us with her wonders to feel awe, compassion, and responsibility. Once a man has realized his fundamental oneness with reality, he cannot avoid feeling his essential kinship with other men. But this sense of a unity which embraces nature and mankind is not merely a sublime concept. It is a demand, a call to creative comradeship with the universal Spirit in the removal of all that obstructs the actualization of communion. According to the mystical faith of Tagore, the awareness that reality is One is an invitation to participate in the divine work of creative reconciliation. Through the abilities, talents, and aspirations of each distinct person, the divine poet composes his epic. His work must continue until every potentiality has been achieved, every goal attained, every purpose harmonized, every injustice rectified, every banality transformed into beauty. Through the gifts of joy and love, he lures each of us toward self-fulfillment within the all-encompassing community. He draws each person out of the tragic self-isolation which sets man against man, man against nature, man against himself. At the core of each man's being the divine artist discloses the unique potential, the personal direction, by which the finite individual may attain his true being within a universal creativity.

TAGORE'S RELIGIOUS IRRELIGION

Rabindranath Tagore was an irreligious man. He rejected the dogmas, ceremonies, and laws of traditional religion; avoided the holy places; ignored the holy men. He despised the self-righteousness and complacency which prompted his countrymen to declare their "spiritual superiority" over the materialistic West. He loathed the superstition, inhumanity, and prejudice nurtured by institutional Hinduism. Nor was he satisfied by the contemporary liberalism of his father's Brahmo Samaj or his friend Gandhi's political activism. Ethics and politics may be wonderful pursuits, but they are not religious. Unless they spring from the transforming power of man's acceptance of his partnership with the divine, they are doomed to produce divisiveness, conflict, and disaster. For the beginning and end of all human efforts must be the realization of the primal One which energizes, unites, and judges. According to Tagore, neither Indian politics nor Hindu religiosity can be considered exemplars of the divine-human comradeship.

And yet, no contemporary figure has been more passionately religious and distinctively Hindu than Rabindranath Tagore. For his career is itself a thorough internalizing, a personifying, of the fundamental transforming insights which gave birth to Hinduism. Tagore demonstrates that the way to be a contemporary Hindu is personally to re-experience, re-live, and re-present the discoveries of the ancient forest sages responsible for the Upanishads. The life of Tagore is paradigmatic of a possibility which is seldom imagined by the critics of traditional religion. The reform of a religion is accomplished neither by immersing it in socio-political dilemmas nor by pointing out the contradictions between affirmation and performance. Vital reform begins with vital individuals who instantiate, exemplify, and reproduce living experiences. The traditions of even the most corrupt institutional religions are clues which we ignore at our peril. The test of even the best religious structures is the presence of transforming power and creative persons. The dynamic and productive irreligion of Rabindranath Tagore testifies eloquently to that pearl of great price *hidden* in all religions.

NOTES

¹ C. F. Andrews, "An Essay on the Bengal Renaissance" in Rabindranath Tagore, *Letters to a Friend* (New York: Macmillan Company, 1929), p. 13.

² Dewan Behadur K. S. Ramaswami Sastri, "Tagore and the Indian Renaissance" in *Gurudev Tagore*, R. Narasimhan, ed. (Bombay: V. Kulkarni, 1946), p. 122.

³ Quoted by D. S. Sarma, *Studies in the Renaissance of Hinduism in the Nineteenth and Twentieth Centuries* (Benares: Benares Hindu University, 1944), p. 350. Sarma's work is the most important single volume on the Indian Renaissance.

⁴ R. Tagore, *The Religion of Man* (Boston: Beacon Press, 1961), p. 91.

⁵ *Ibid.*, p. 93.

⁶ Tagore, *My Reminiscences* (London: Macmillan, 1917), p. 217.

⁷ Tagore, *The Religion of Man*, pp. 93–94.

⁸ Tagore, *Gitanjali, Song Offerings* (New York: Macmillan Company, 1912), p. 64 (hereafter cited as *Gitanjali*).

⁹ *The Religion of Man*, p. 96.

¹⁰ *Ibid.*

¹¹ *Ibid.*, p. 99.

¹² *Ibid.*, p. 100.

¹³ *Gitanjali*, p. 46.

14 Tagore, *Creative Unity* (New York: Macmillan Company, 1922), p. 78.

15 *Ibid.*, p. 80.

16 Sarma, *op. cit.*, p. 388.

17 *Gitanjali*, pp. 8–9.

18 Quoted by Sarma, *op. cit.*, p. 368.

19 *Gitanjali*, p. 64.

20 Sarma, *op. cit.*, p. 396.

21 Quoted by Sarma, *op. cit.*, pp. 400–401.

22 *Gitanjali*, p. 23.

Recommended Readings

The following is a brief list of works recommended for the interested general reader. It is not intended as a bibliography of items cited or consulted in the present volume; but is limited to work which I consider essentially helpful to the serious nonscholar. Note: "Pb." indicates a paperback edition.

BOOKS ABOUT SEVERAL RELIGIONS

Ninian Smart, *The Religious Experience of Mankind*. New York: Charles Scribner's Sons, 1968 (pb.).

A superb one-author, one-volume history of mankind's religious experience. Smart is fair, judicious, and sane. Any defects may be traced to the ambitious scope of the undertaking. It simply is not possible for one man to digest, analyze, and synthesize the data available to contemporary historians of religion. But Smart, who is basically a philosopher of religion, succeeds to a remarkable extent. No other one-author effort evidences greater sympathy, interpretive skill, or humanitarian breadth.

R. C. Zaehner, et al, *The Concise Encyclopedia of Living Faiths*. Boston: Beacon Press, 1967 (pb.).

Separate essays on the world's major religions by leading western scholars. This enormous paperback is an invaluable reference tool. Although I find the category-structure of the volume (i.e., Eastern mysticism versus Hebraic theism) less than adequate, there is no better one-volume work. The over-all quality, readability, and scholarship are uniformly high. But why, we must ask, were the chapters on Hinduism, Jainism, Buddhism, Shinto, Confucianism, and Taoism not written by Oriental scholars?

R. C. Chalmers and John A. Irving, eds., *The Meaning of Life in Five Great Religions*. Philadelphia: the Westminster Press, 1966 (pb.).

An essay on Hinduism by a Hindu; on Buddhism by a Buddhist; on Islam by a Muslim; etc. Unfortunately the general quality is low. Nevertheless the conception is praiseworthy.

Wing-tsit Chan, Isma-il Ragi al Farugi, Joseph M. Kitagawa, P. T. Raju, eds., *The Great Asian Religions* (New

York: Macmillan Company, 1969). A one-volume collection of major Oriental religions compiled by scholars
who are both scholars and Asiatics.

GENERAL WORKS

Marshall McLuhan and Quentin Fiore, *The Medium is
the Massage*: An Inventory of Effects. New York: Bantam
Books, 1967 (pb.). Wow! Need I say more?

Thomas F. O'Dea, *The Sociology of Religion*. Englewood
Cliffs, New Jersey, 1966 (pb.).
    A superb introduction to much important literature on
a variety of topics: religion and society, religious experience,
religious institutions, religions and magic, etc. The material
is not well integrated.

Mircea Eliade, *The Sacred and the Profane*. New York:
Harcourt, Brace and Company, Inc., 1959. (There is a
pb. edition published by Harper Torchbooks which has
gone out of print.)
    This important volume by the leading phenomenologist
of religion is aptly described by the publisher as an essay
on "the nature of religion . . . , the significance of religious
myth, symbolism, and ritual within life and culture."

Joachim Wach, *The Comparative Study of Religions,*
edited with an introduction by Joseph M. Kitagawa. New
York: Columbia University Press, 1958 (pb.).

The late Professor Wach was probably the most significant contributor to the scientific study of religions. This
volume presents the guidelines for future investigations.
Unfortunately these essays read like unexpanded lecture
notes.

HINDUISM

Madeleine Biardeau, *India,* translated by F. Carter. New
York: The Viking Press, 1960. A Vista Book (pb.).

A remarkable introduction to Indian life, culture, and
religion by a French traveller. Miss Biardeau's book is intel-
ligent, sympathetic, and critical. This illustrated travel guide
puts most scholarly texts to shame. The perfect book for
the beginner.

R. C. Zaehner, *Hinduism.* New York: Oxford University
Press, 1966 (pb.).

An excellent short introduction to the history of Indian
religious thought from period of the Vedas to the present
day.

K. M. Sen, *Hinduism: The World's Oldest Faith.* Baltimore, Md.: Pelican Books, 1961 (pb.).

Similar to Zaehner's book but much more concise. Sen, an associate of Tagore's at Santiniketan, adds selections from the major Hindu scriptures to his all too brief account of the development of Hinduism.

Rabindranath Tagore, *Gitanjali, Song Offerings*. London: Macmillan & Co. Ltd., 1962.
Tagore received the Nobel Prize for this collection of "song offerings." The themes are universal; the voice distinctly Indian.

―――. *A Tagore Reader*, ed., Amiya Chakravarty. Boston Beacon Press, 1968 (pb.).
A convenient introduction to the thought of a towering spiritual giant.

The Upanishads: Breath of the Eternal. The Principal Texts Selected and Translated from the Original Sanskrit by Swami Prabhavananda and Frederick Manchester. New York: New American Library, 1964 (pb.).
The most influential of the major Hindu scriptures.

The Bhagavad Gita. Translated from the Sanskrit with an Introduction by Juan Mascaró. Baltimore, Md.: Penguin Books, 1965 (pb.).
This epic poem of King Arjuna's dialogue with the Lord Krishna on the eve of battle is the Hindu layman's Bible.

These eighty pages are probably the most profound and moving of all the religious writings of mankind.

BUDDHISM

Edward Conze, *Buddhism: Its Essence and Development*. New York: Harper Torchbooks, 1959 (pb.).
Not easy reading but the best general introduction.

Walpola Rahula, *What the Buddha Taught*. New York: Grove Press, Inc., 1962 (pb.).
The only worthwhile book on Buddhism as a viable philosophy of life. I agree fully with the author, a Ceylonese monk, that most previous books about Buddhism "have been written by those who are not really competent, or who bring to their task misleading assumptions derived from other religions, which must misinterpret and misrepresent their subject."

The Teachings of the Compassionate Buddha. Basic Buddhist Scriptures edited with commentary by E. A. Burtt. New York: New American Library. 1963 (pb.).
An indispensable collection of basic religious and ethical writings. Burtt is a most trustworthy guide.

THE MODERN
RELIGIOUS PREDICAMENT

Rodney Stark and Charles Y. Glock, *American Piety: The Nature of Religious Commitment* (Patterns of Religious Commitment: Volume 1). Berkeley and Los Angeles: University of California Press, 1968.

The Huntley-Brinkley of American sociology of religion provide the hard data for predictions of the future of religion. This is not an encouraging report. Good!

The Hippies. By the Correspondents of *Time.* Edited by Joe David Brown. New York: Time Incorporated, 1967 (pb.).

The material that was left over from a *Time* feature. Vital documentation of a fading fad which will be investigated again and again during the next hundred years.

William Braden. *The Private Sea, LSD and the Search for God.* New York: Bantam Books, 1968 (pb.).

A remarkable examination of LSD, New Theology, humanistic psychology, and the attractions of Oriental spirituality by a sensitive reporter. There is a feeling of amateurism and inconclusiveness in much of the book. Yet no one has more successfully called attention to the religious implications of the drug cults or better delineated the shape of things to come.

Samuel Sandmel, *We Jews and You Christians*. Philadelphia: J. B. Lippincott Company, 1967.

An analysis of Jewish-Christian relations in the light of the secular threat to religion. This book has received little attention from either Christians or Jews. It deserves careful consideration and much discussion.

Leonard Cohen, *Spice-Box of Earth*. New York: Bantam Books, 1968.

Most of these poems are included in Cohen's *Selected Poems*. However, I have no particular admiration for the remainder. "Spice-Box" must be read aloud (preferably with guitar accompaniment) to a special friend. For a real treat, intersperse selections from Tagore's *Gitanjali*. If your betrothed does not appreciate the effort, break the engagement.

Paul Tillich, *The Future of Religions*. Edited by Jerald C. Brauer. New York: Harper & Row, 1966.

Contains four important essays by Tillich dealing with space exploration, the myth of endless human progress, the significance of non-Christian religions for Christian theology, etc. (I note that John Updike chose a selection from this volume for the frontispiece of Couples.) It is my conviction that these essays form a prolegomena to the future of Christian thought.

And, finally, without further comment, may I commend three books which speak eloquently of the American condition?

Eldridge Cleaver, *Soul on Ice*. New York: Delta Books, 1968 (pb.).

Malcolm X, *The Autobiography of Malcolm X*. New York: Grove Press, Inc., 1966 (pb.).

Lenny Bruce, *How to Talk Dirty and Influence People: An Autobiography*. Chicago, Ill.: Playboy Press, 1966 (pb.).